RURAL DIVERSIFICATION

by

Peter A B Prag

MA FRICS

2000

Divisions of Reed Business Information

First published 2000

ISBN 0 7282 0331 6

Estates Gazette
151 Wardour Street, London W1V 4BN

Typeset by Amy Boyle, Rochester, Kent
Printed and bound by Bell and Bain Ltd, Glasgow

Contents

Preface and Acknowledgements

The idea for this book was born in the autumn of 1998. Diversification was hardly a new phenomenon in the countryside at the time, but the pressure on farm incomes was becoming increasingly serious. The cereal harvest was achieving dismal prices for the second successive year, milk prices were falling too and the livestock sector was in the grip of rising regulatory costs and disappearing margins. Across the entire agricultural industry only the potato market appeared to be showing any sort of buoyancy. This raised the questions: Could things go on as they were? What were the alternatives?

Since then, even the potato prices have fallen and there has been little improvement elsewhere. The only respite seemed to be in a further slight fall in interest rates, which would have reduced overall costs for some farmers and allowed the banks to remain calm in the face of a continuing decline in incomes and little prospect for any recovery. Faced with these circumstances, diversification is worth considering as a potential remedy. During 1999 the NFU published a survey which showed that nearly two-thirds of farmers in Britain had diversified their incomes and were involved with over 150 different types of non-farming occupations. There would certainly seem to be many opportunities, but the fact that they are so varied and numerous and in most cases so different to the traditional business of farming means that it is not easy to know how best to embark upon such a venture. The aim of this book is to offer guidance on the general issues involved and to provide some practical pointers.

Inevitably this covers a wide range of topics and I have been fortunate in being able to consult with experts in these different fields. In this connection, I would like to record my thanks to the following: Andrew Burgess of Humberts Planning, Michael Fellingham of Penningtons, Peter FitzGerald of Wilsons, Jeremy Lewis of Grant Thornton, Nigel Talbot-Ponsonby of Humberts Leisure and Richard Waters of Barclays Bank.

Peter A. B. Prag
December 1999

Chapter One

Introduction

Farms and estates have to face up to constantly changing circumstances, not just in terms of profitability, but in other important aspects too. In addition to a financial downturn across the country there have also been pressures of both a political and social nature as well as changes within the basic structure of land management. These factors are all bound to affect agricultural businesses. To ensure continued profitability or even survival, each factor needs to be countered by one means or another.

The financial situation has been well recorded over recent years, with its causes rooted in the Common Agricultural Policy (CAP), the strength of sterling and the impact of ongoing negotiations for the World Trade Agreement (WTA), as well as particular problems of weather or disease, such as BSE. The political influence is equally pervasive, with a growing emphasis on environmental and ecological measures and on the needs and rural perceptions of the general public. Meanwhile, agricultural businesses have become increasingly regulated from both the European Commission and national planning and safety measures. The social implications are felt in rural areas with a decrease in the number of farmers and a rise in their average ages, as younger people are turning to alternative livelihoods. The structural change manifests itself in fewer long term tenancies; a greater use of short term farming arrangements and a trend towards larger farm units.

The combined effect of all these factors on the agricultural sector tends to be negative, resulting in reduced returns and a need to recoup one's losses. The situation is particularly crucial in a rural context, where there is a long-standing commitment to the farm, whether owned or tenanted, especially as it is often a family home as well as a place of business.

Furthermore, there is every indication that throughout Britain this trend can only get worse. It is widely accepted that the CAP is unsustainable even in its present form, let alone when expanded, as it must be, to absorb the first tranche of central European countries. The harsh reality seems to be that one day the present system of subsidised support will have to be wound down. Farmers will then have to survive in the open market of world prices. For some of the most vulnerable there may still be financial assistance of some kind funded by national governments in order to maintain certain landscapes or communities, such as those found in the remoter upland areas. For most, however, it will be clear that their business will have to change if it is to continue under these new conditions.

In political terms, it has to be recognised that a reduction in agricultural support will lead to fewer farms – or certainly to fewer full time farms. It may be that the total number of holdings will not in fact radically decline but more will become part time businesses, either in the hands of the present occupiers or of new owners who were not previously farmers. There is already a strong tradition throughout much of Continental Europe of part time holdings. This derived from the Napoleonic code of law whereby land passed to a wider number of heirs than in Britain, where the rule of primogeniture has tended to apply. As a result, in Continental Europe land holdings became smaller over the generations to an extent that even in stronger economic times many were no longer viable as self-contained units and could only be run in conjunction with some other source of income. Now we are seeing in many areas, including Britain, a trend where people who already have a commercial occupation wish to combine it with a rural environment and are ready to take on a small farm to achieve this. The fact that the number of full time agricultural holdings is declining will not therefore inevitably lead to the countryside becoming depopulated. In the more remote areas it is likely that fewer people will remain living and working on the land. Elsewhere one can expect to see a radical social change as farms and other rural properties are acquired by a more diversified and mobile community.

Meanwhile present day farmers still have to face a change in their financial positions. There will come a time for many when, even after introducing all possible economies and improvements in efficiency, the farm will become unprofitable. This will arise when income can no longer meet the overheads, whether in the form of bank borrowing or rent or simply the outright cost of running the farm and providing for the family's needs. In any case, something will have to be done. Where bank borrowings need to be reduced some adjustments are often possible, through refinancing or the sale of part of the asset such as a surplus cottage. Such measures tend however to be only of a short term nature. For tenant farmers, if the holding is no longer viable, one would expect the rent to be reduced until it could return to profit. In reality, however, this has rarely occurred while the market remains under pressure from some quarters as other farmers are determined to gain additional land so as to improve the efficiency of their businesses through economies of scale.

The answer then will be to find a source of income independently of the farm. The concept of combining one's farming with a part time job elsewhere is however often difficult to realise. In many rural areas suitable employment may not be available or only at a distance that would involve too much time and cost in travel in order to continue to maintain what had after all been a full time occupation in running the farm. There is a limit to anyone's energies when faced with doing the milking or the feeding or the lambing before and after a long day working for example in a factory. Also, however competent someone may have been as a farmer they may not have the ability or the aptitude to become a wage earner elsewhere.

If the necessary extra income cannot be found, then the next and rather final step that suggests itself is to give up the farm. For those who own their farms this is at least a viable option, even if often a rather distressing one, and the net proceeds of the sale of the property may well be sufficient to provide for an alternative future. For tenants of course the position is very different; whilst there can be timely opportunities for negotiating a cash settlement with the landlord, in many other instances there will be little left to a tenant other than the net receipts from the sale of live and deadstock.

A disposal of the business need not however mean having to leave the farm. There are now many ways in which the land can be let or contracted out to a neighbour or a farming company. Utilising their more efficient scale of operations, such outside parties are often able to pay a higher return than that which the incumbent farmer was previously earning from the holding even under the increasingly difficult circumstances of the time. Meanwhile, the original farmer has also been able to raise cash and reduce or extinguish borrowings through the sale of all stock and machinery. Even with the advantageous arrangements now available for creating contracts or Farm Business Tenancies (FBTs), this may not always offer a feasible solution. A tenant may be prohibited by the terms of the original lease from subletting the land and even where this can be done, whether by tenant or owner, it is not easy to remain living in the farmhouse when someone else is farming the land and using the buildings.

When these various alternatives seem so difficult to implement, it may be that the best, and possibly only, answer will be in developing an alternative income source from the farm itself through the introduction of a new venture. The most common and pressing cause of such diversification arises from a need to counter a downward trend in income, as described. It would appear furthermore to relate predominantly to the smaller farms that have the greater difficulty in competing in the present market. But the situation is more complex than this. To begin with the definition of a small farm has been changing in recent times; what would have been a viable unit in a father's day may no longer be viable for the son's generation. 30 years' ago a cereal farm of, say, 150 hectares or a dairy unit of 50 cows would each have been comfortably sufficient but neither could now be expected to provide a proper family income. As regards diversification the larger farms of whatever size can also find good cause to introduce new non-agricultural ventures. In doing so, they may be taking advantage not only of their own particular business strengths but also exploiting a positive market change. In business terms, these bigger holdings are likely to have a stronger capital base from which to fund the new enterprise, whether with bank borrowings or from internal resources. They are likely too to have a more sophisticated management expertise than their smaller counterparts, making it easier to develop new concepts. The rationale for doing so may be initially to find a means of covering rising overheads or to plan for future pressures, but it can also be to expand what is already a successful business, or in response to another factor: the changing pattern of the countryside.

There can of course also be positive reasons for undertaking such a change in direction, with farmers and landowners taking advantage of new demands and developments in the countryside. There has after all been a remarkable switch in emphasis in recent times, away from the post war era when food production was the prime purpose of land to a situation now in which the issues of conservation and recreation can be of equal importance. To most farmers these current policies may seem to bring just more potential problems: of increased regulation leading as often as not to reduced profitability, or of wider instances of trespass and other interference. Others may recognise them as a new opportunity, benefiting, for example, from additional grants and subsidies linked to environmental schemes. The growing number of people coming to the country, whether as visitors or residents, can be viewed as a potential new crop to be harvested through providing both residential and commercial accommodation or offering services such as farm shops or riding stables. The introduction of schemes of this kind will often involve new uses for land and buildings.

As incomes declined over the past few years, everyone will already have been checking the efficiency of their business and making the adjustments and improvements that they felt were necessary and feasible. In most cases these would be in the field of agriculture itself and therefore helped by being still within the farmer's existing expertise. Although new management structures and cropping systems need to be properly planned and budgeted, much of the necessary information is relatively readily assimilated from one's existing advisers, neighbours or from conferences or shows. It is different, however, when this involves the introduction of a new business venture. The essential information may be less readily obtainable and the planning then requires not only the ability to assess the projected financial viability but also the ability to identify particular opportunities and finding the means of implementing them successfully.

In many cases, full consideration is required to ascertain how farm assets might be used to best advantage and their proper potential, be they owned, rented or merely contracted.

The purpose of this book is to point the way towards achieving such diversification and to outline the factors that need to be considered. There is an almost endless range of possibilities and it would be impossible to give specific answers to all these various situations, but it is useful to establish the general principles that tend to be involved and define the procedures that need to be followed. The book does contain a directory of organisations from where more detailed advice may be obtained on individual types of enterprise.

In the present climate, it is likely that almost every farmer and landowner will need to explore new opportunities and to go through this exercise, for reasons that are introduced in the next chapter.

Chapter Two

Reasons for Diversification

Rural diversification is not a new concept. For many years one has seen land and buildings being converted to a variety of uses. There will have been a number of possible reasons why such schemes were implemented. These reasons still apply today, although the overall circumstances have changed significantly in that virtually all farm businesses have been affected by an ongoing decline in agricultural returns and need to review their positions. In assessing the grounds for embarking upon a new alternative venture, it is important first to define the different factors leading up to such a step being taken and also weighing up the other available options. Each individual case will of course have its own specific set of circumstances, but there are also some basic principles that apply to all. It is useful to consider these at the outset.

2.1 Checking the decline in farm income

There have always been years when farm incomes have fallen from their previous levels, whether due to a difficult and disappointing harvest, illness within a flock or herd or market fluctuation. Traditionally, such factors could be expected to improve within the following year or two and the farm business would return to profitability. These temporary downturns might therefore have been met with little more than a renegotiation of overdraft facilities, a curb on private drawings or the postponement of some investment in new equipment. In some situations, however, it might have encouraged a review of the existing farming practices and led to certain improvements or rationalisation being made so as to increase efficiency. These would be likely to embrace a wide range of management considerations which may by now have become almost routine, such as reviewing the crop varieties or the use of agrochemicals or of feed compounds. These could probably be implemented with little or no change to the overall business structure of the farm.

But alongside such seasonal fluctuations there has of course also been an economic trend in recent years that has made it harder for many smaller farms to remain viable. The relative fall in prices and subsidies against the inflationary rise in production costs has meant that overheads have to be spread over larger units. Equipment has to be worked more efficiently over a bigger acreage or a greater head of stock has to be operated by a smaller number of employees. Milking 50 cows on 30 hectares or growing cereals on 100 hectares is unlikely anymore to provide a financial return for a full-time farmer. It is unlikely too that this shortfall could be redressed merely by increasing efficiency through taking the kind of measures mentioned above.

In these situations, as with some larger mixed farms, financial performance will probably only be improved through making structural changes to the business. On the mixed farm it may be that a livestock enterprise has to be abandoned and the sheep or cattle sold, the grassland then sold or let out on a sharefarming or grazing agreement. With the smaller arable unit, it could be more efficient to employ contractors rather than using one's own labour and machinery or, again, to let out the land to neighbours. In either case, capital is released and labour costs are reduced, but this latter saving presupposes that it is acceptable to make employees redundant. In the former case, where livestock is sold, buildings may become redundant too and if some of the staff leave then their houses might become vacant as well.

In these examples steps have been taken to reduce costs. Initially on the grounds that the existing business could not survive without such rationalisation and that, when implemented, it should be more feasible to continue farming, albeit with fewer enterprises and employees on the farm. The question then arises as to whether the empty cattle buildings or the redundant staff could be re-utilised in some other income earning capacity. This might be either because even after restructuring the farm business is unable to produce a sufficient return and some additional income needs to be earned or because the redundant resources are seen as an opportunity that ought to be exploited. In either case, diversification is being introduced, although from two very different angles which have a fundamental bearing on how the end result is to be achieved.

2.2 Supplementing inadequate income

This arises in a situation where the existing farm enterprise is no longer able to generate sufficient income, even after the implementation of whatever improvements or efficiencies may have been available. The only answer appears to be to diversify and introduce a new venture. There is a danger here that this new scheme will be undertaken primarily because some alternative has to be found. In these circumstances it is possible that sufficient regard is not paid to whether it is potentially profitable or suitable to the farmer's abilities and interests or indeed to the property and its locality. It might be an exaggeration to describe such a move as an act of desperation. However it is harder to devise a successful project when starting from the relatively negative stance that something simply has to be found, than when starting from one of the more positive approaches described in later sections. For example, where a beef or dairy enterprise has been given up, the farmer will realise that the old calf pens are empty and available for some other use. Having a low eaves height and limited internal working space, the most immediate answer might be conversion to loose boxes for use as a livery stable. If no one on the farm has any interest or liking for horses, it would be harder to succeed than if it were something with which they had some affinity. Also, if the area is one where many horse owners have their own paddock and stable, then the level of demand could be disappointing and unprofitable.

This scenario where one is effectively forced into finding some new alternative source of income is not entirely negative, as it does at least initiate the whole process of looking for an improvement. It will, however, require a particularly careful and thorough approach if one is to weigh up all the balancing factors correctly.

2.3 Exploiting an opportunity or ability

In this situation, the new venture has been identified in a more positive manner in that it is something that the farmer feels he could do well and for which the property and its location are be well suited. The income situation may be equally pressing as in the previous example, but it has the advantage that there is more of a reason for proceeding with the diversification than pure financial necessity. It still needs to be carefully researched and, indeed, there is a danger that the individual's own enthusiasm could be too positive and distort the outcome! None the less, one can see someone who is, for example, a keen shot and well known within local shooting circles would be better suited to setting up a clay pigeon shoot than someone who was less familiar with the sport.

In many cases, it tends to be assumed that where a new and secondary venture is introduced on to a farm it is because the core business of agriculture is no longer sufficiently profitable and needs to be supplemented by this means. In reality, it can as easily be in response to new opportunities arising from changes in the way we live or in the foods we eat or in our use of leisure time. Such situations can produce a direct financial return and may therefore be exploited even when the farming business is going well and appears not to need any alternative income stream. Examples of this will have been seen over the years in the expansion of the organic food sector or the increase in golf courses as farmers and landowners have responded to new demands. Occasionally, the financial incentive will come from Government sources in the form of grants rather than commercial market forces, as in the case of the Countryside Stewardship Scheme, for example.

An opportunity may offer itself also through a new use of existing farm buildings. As agricultural practices are modernised and adapted to meet changing circumstances, some of the older buildings may become redundant. Although too small or impractical for new methods or machinery, these barns may still represent a valuable resource if put to use for a different and non-agricultural purpose.

2.4 Planning future expansion

It may be that the existing farm business is viable within its present context but that there is a need to increase its income in order to meet some changing circumstance such as a son or daughter coming into the family business. It incorporates many of the factors outlined in the previous cases in that there is a financial need to find some additional activity. There may be a special ability within the family that ought to be used. In this example, however, the pressure to supplement income may not be quite so urgent as when the farm is already making regular losses. By being still profitable, it will attract a more helpful stance from the banks and it will be possible also to wait until the right solution has been found – the son or daughter can easily take a year or so working elsewhere and gaining experience! Often when a business is being expanded so as to include the younger generation, they bring with them new ideas and abilities which may be more readily tuned to new ventures than that of their parents whose experience and outlook is more deeply rooted in traditional farming. Youthful imagination and enthusiasm may be a useful ingredient when embarking on a new enterprise, although it may also need some extra attention when securing finance, as mentioned in section 5.1.2.

2.5 Arranging joint ventures

The grounds for potential diversification which have been considered so far are ones that would be instigated by farmers or landowners who are looking for ways to branch out from their core business, whether for defensive or opportunist reasons. So many of these schemes will have little to do with traditional agriculture and will require a new and different expertise, while using however the landed property as its basis. One can see then that there may well be occasions when someone who has experience in running a diversified business of this kind will be searching for a site on which to develop it. One possible solution would be for such an entrepreneur to enter into a collaboration with a landowner, whereby the latter contributes the property while the former undertakes to develop and manage the agreed scheme. These partnerships or joint ventures need to be carefully arranged, as mentioned further in section 9.1.5. Although the landowner may not have to be personally capable of organising the new business, he will still have to be fully advised on such matters as investment costs, potential returns and the appropriate legal structures.

2.6 Facing changing circumstances

The emphasis has so far been on ways in which farmers might seek to counter a steady fall in income or the loss of viability of the smaller units. This is understandable given the concern that these trends have caused throughout the industry, but there has meanwhile been another area of change within the countryside in that there is ever increasing development in rural districts. Another variant to the earlier cases considered above may therefore arise when circumstances change in the vicinity of the property, due perhaps to a change in either local or national Government policies.

Diversification may then offer itself even though the farmer or landowner had not previously had reason to consider it. New development in the vicinity may change the emphasis of local planning, so that a farmyard scheme that in the past would not have gained consent nor been perceived as viable would now be likely to do so. A new road diversion or additional housing in the area could create such opportunities with an increased population, an easier traffic flow and a changed commitment on the part of the local authority. Planning issues are dealt with further in chapter 8, but as a general principle it should be noted that the question of whether an agricultural property might be successfully converted to another use could depend on events occurring away from the farm and not always rely solely upon an initiative being taken on that property alone.

Chapter Three

Initial Analysis

3.1 Introduction

Having decided therefore, for whichever reason, to introduce a particular form of diversification, it can then be rather difficult and daunting to know how to begin. At this initial stage, it can be as well to check out a whole range of factors in brief outline so as to establish what is likely to be involved and which aspects are likely to be crucial and to warrant more detailed investigation at the outset.

In most cases it best to start with an appraisal of the existing enterprises, looking at the current and budgeted returns and at production costs. Before introducing a new venture it is as well to know exactly what resources are available and what effect any changes might have on the present income. It will also be important to identify the wider consequences that these might have on, for example, the employment of staff or the continued use of land and buildings.

In the first instance, solutions will no doubt have been sought that would allow the present enterprises to continue but on a more profitable basis. The next step would then be to consider taking additional measures that might however involve a degree of structural change while still continuing with the same business ventures. It may be decided, for example, to use contractors in order save on overheads for staff and machinery. This might well improve profitability and appear to keep the farm unaltered, but will result also in employees no longer being required for their previous tasks. As a consequence they would face the unpleasant prospect of redundancy, unless of course an alternative viable occupation were to be found for them on the farm, implying the introduction of a new venture or in other words a form of diversification.

At a further stage, the analysis may recognise that the farm business itself needs to be changed and that perhaps a loss making enterprise should be given up, as in the case of a mixed farm when a beef herd is sold. In this instance the financial remedy will release not only the staff time spent in running the herd but also other resources such as the grassland and the covered yards and dutch barns. The answer may yet be to make the employees redundant and to let out the grazing and possibly even the buildings too, but there could also be an opportunity to reuse all these facilities for a different purpose. This may be another agricultural venture where, for example, an exotic breed of animal like ostriches or llamas would effectively replace the former beef cattle. It could also be a non-farming business which might utilize either just the buildings for storage or light manufacturing or take over some of the land as well. This might still be for grazing, in conjunction with an equestrian enterprise, or for a completely different use such as a site for car boot sales or motor bike scrambling.

In both scenarios, there will be a need to take a new approach and to gain new expertise. With the exotic livestock, however, this will still follow similar procedures to those used with the cattle, namely feeding, rearing and marketing. Whereas a non-farming use would involve a less familiar management function. In the former case too the buildings may not require major change or expenditure, whereas the non-farming occupation might necessitate further building work and investment.

The order in which one begins to make this initial analysis may vary according to the circumstances of each case, depending on the nature of the venture, the farmer's situation and the reasons for which the new enterprise has been mooted in the first place. In each case, however it is likely to involve a preliminary financial appraisal, an assessment of the physical features of the property and the practicalities of introducing the new enterprise, and some enquiry into planning regulations.

3.2 Financial

3.2.1 *The existing enterprise*

It is likely that any new and alternative enterprise will be introduced alongside an existing business rather than replace it entirely. The ongoing performance of that core business will therefore continue to be important, particularly during the initial period when most new ventures will still be in a development stage and not yet showing any profits. It is useful then to begin by looking at the past farm accounts and reviewing the current budget and cash flow. Most forms of diversification will impact upon the existing business by using some part of the land and buildings or other resources. Even where it is thought that there will be no such conflict, such as when only a disused building is to be given over, one must weigh up the demands that may still be made on management time or on farm staff. Only if that workforce is at present under-utilized would it be fair to assume that there would not be any draw upon the farm business. In most cases, however, there will be many areas where the budget for the existing business will have to be revised before one can assess the additional return that is likely to come from the new venture.

This might be illustrated by an example where on a mainly arable farm it is proposed that a beef suckler herd should be given up and that a livery business introduced instead. There are barns that would then become available for conversion into stables and pasture land that could be used for grazing by horses. This may seem logical and straightforward but there are some financial considerations that still need to be addressed. The costs of converting the buildings and upgrading fencing are basic issues that will clearly need to be assessed at the outset and which are dealt with in more detail in a later section. At this stage, one needs to revise the annual budget and in doing so must remove from it the income from the annual sale of calves or finished cattle and from any premiums that may be received. Against this there is likely to be a saving in costs of feed and vet's bills. The proceeds from the disposal of the suckler cows themselves will presumably appear as a capital item in the balance sheet. One then needs to ask how the time that had been spent by someone in looking after the cattle will now be accounted for. Is that person going to be working with the livery business and if so would they be competent or suitable to do so? If not, is their time going to remain a fixed cost against the farm enterprise even though it no longer benefits from the income from the suckler herd? Otherwise if that person were now to become redundant, has an allowance been made for the statutory payments that would be due?

Furthermore, the arable enterprise may have previously benefited from a source of fertiliser from the suckler herd, either by rotational grazing on leys around the farm or from being winter housed on straw. The livery stables are likely to use other bedding materials than straw so that the farm will now need to dispose of the straw either by sale, which might produce a small income, or by incorporation, which would be an added cost. It may be also that the livery business will need grazing close to the buildings and that the former cattle pastures, which might have been off lying, will become available for arable cultivation. These old pastures may not be so well suited to cereal production and the overall performance of the farm could be affected accordingly.

This example is by no means comprehensive and there will be further issues that need to be accounted for and which will be dealt with in later sections. For the present however, it should be clear that before part of a farm can be released for a new enterprise one must take a lateral approach and identify all the implications for the remaining core business.

3.2.2 *Capital values*

The initial assessment can extend beyond the issue of how the farm's income and overheads could be affected and may have to be applied also to the question of its capital value. Where for example a traditional farmyard is being redeveloped into commercial premises, the future rental income would be estimated and assessed as a return on the anticipated cost of the building work. Given that the old barns were no longer of any significant use to the farm, one may assume that there would be no consequent loss in income to account for and that proposed scheme would therefore be deemed to be viable. It is possible however that the longer term value of the remaining property would be adversely affected by the new development. The original farmyard may not have been very practical for modern farming purposes but it could well be picturesque and add to the charm of the main house. Once those buildings have been separated out and given over to a commercial use, the house would become less attractive as a result and therefore less valuable.

If the current owners are not intending to sell the house in the foreseeable future, they may consider this to be a rather hypothetical issue and argue that they will be more than compensated by the resulting rental income. None the less, such diminution in capital value should be recognised when planning the development, particularly where capital costs are being incurred in carrying out the conversion work. This can be particularly relevant when the new scheme is being financed by a loan or mortgage secured against the main property, as discussed further in section 5.1.2. In many cases the conversion work will, when completed, add to the value of the property as a whole. This is not only reassuring to the owner but can also make it easier to justify the investment and to raise any finance that may be required.

3.2.3 *The new venture*

The introduction of any new business venture will need a full financial analysis, as detailed in chapter 5. Much of this will probably have to be done in full at an early stage in the project, although before embarking upon complex calculations it may be helpful first to have assessed just the essential factors.

The basic questions that need to be asked can initially be reduced to very straight forward format:

- How much will it cost to establish?
- What income will it produce when completed?
- How long will it take until that income is received?
- What regular out goings will be incurred in running the new business?
- How reliable will that income stream be in the future?

It is difficult to estimate the cost of development works without going into detail and taking professional advice, although it may be possible to produce a very approximate figure for initial budgeting purposes by using the standard costs produced by MAFF and by the SAC Buildings Design Unit, Aberdeen, and reproduced in *The Farm Management Pocketbook* by John Nix. At this stage it may also be as much a matter of identifying all the areas where such expenditure would be incurred. For example, where a new building is to be erected one may well start by working out what size it needs to be and then apply the appropriate standard cost per square metre. Such figures will not however allow for the expense of getting the site prepared for the new construction, which could be quite extensive especially if this were to involve the demolition of an existing building. Other such instances arise when a new access has to be constructed or some provision made for rehousing stock or equipment previously kept on that site. Many such features can be anticipated just by taking a logical approach to all the issues that are likely to arise when implementing a new scheme, but others may only become evident as part of discussions for planning or building and environmental regulations: see chapter 8.

A rudimentary initial estimate of income can be derived by working out the quantity of material being sold and multiplying it by the price per unit. This principle can be applied to almost every type of venture whether it be the rent for office accommodation or the sale of free-range eggs. This will however produce a figure of gross income and from this will then have to be deducted an item for the cost of management or production. This is less easy to estimate without first doing a comprehensive analysis, although it should be possible to gain a rough indication by assessing the amount of management time that is likely to be involved and the cost of in-puts, such as poultry feed. Once again there may be other factors that need to be identified and then accounted for in addition to the actual costs of production, such as where a higher insurance premium is charged against the farm due to the introduction of a new venture. The sale price per unit can, for this initial purpose, be established by checking what is currently being charged in similar situations that are already in operation.

These preliminary assessments of costs and returns will only give rough approximations of the average anticipated performance. They are unlikely to show the time that may elapse before a full income is received and there may be cases where this will have to be quantified as part of the initial investment. For example, if it were decided to establish a vineyard, one's first analysis would encompass the cost of establishing the vines, in terms of the price of buying the stock and of the labour in planting and tending them during establishment. The return could also be quantified, even if only as a price at which the grapes could be sold to a winery multiplied by the expected yield in tonnes per hectare. What has not however been brought into this basic equation is the time that will elapse until the vines are capable of producing a marketable crop. In the case of a newly planted vineyard, this could be several years during which time the original investment is producing no return but is incurring ongoing management expenses. The initial financial calculation must therefore make allowance for this and the start-up capital might have to include an item to cover interest charges or other drawings during that period. A more comprehensive appraisal, such as is considered in section 5.2, would include a budgeted cash flow to cover this kind of situation and also to accommodate any other delays or distortions in receiving income or in paying for costs.

In the case of a new vineyard it is a physical constraint that prevents one from receiving a full income in the early years, in that the vines take time to become established and to produce a marketable crop of grapes. There may also be situations where such a slow start arises from commercial considerations, such as the difficulties of overcoming competition when starting to sell a product into an established retail market. It is less easy to estimate the time needed for this than it is in the case of the vines. The commercial market forces will vary according to the product and to ever changing circumstances, whereas with a vineyard one can at least find out as a fact how long it will be before a proper harvest can be taken. That said, of course, there will still be an element of uncertainty about how the market may have changed in the meanwhile. Since vines can take three years to become established and a total of six years to reach full production, it is quite possible that prices and outlets will fluctuate during that time.

This illustrates the element of risk referred to in the fourth question posed above as to how reliable the currently budgeted income may be in the future. This is dealt with more fully at a later stage (in section 5.2.1) but for those ventures where it is apparent at the outset that there is uncertainty about future return it may need to be investigated more carefully at the outset.

3.2.4 *Funding*

Most diversification schemes will involve a capital outlay and where this is to be sourced through borrowings, it will be necessary to check at the outset that such funding is available and to work out the annual cost and the best means by which it can be arranged. These procedures are dealt with later in section 5.1.2. If however there is already a loan or mortgage secured against the property, it may be that the consent of the lender is required before any changes are made to that property. The original loan contract may require that such consent be obtained even if the new work were being done without further borrowings. While it is unlikely that there would be any difficulty about this for a scheme that is demonstrably viable, it is as well to check such formalities at an appropriate stage.

3.3 The property

One of the reasons why a new venture may be considered for a farm is that the property itself offers a particular opportunity for doing so. It may be that the farmhouse is larger than that which a modern family now requires or can justify, having been built during periods when several generations would be in the one house, together even with domestic staff. Similarly, there can still be cottages on the property that were needed previously for farm workers but which are now surplus to the farm's requirements as fewer people remain in agriculture or continue to live in houses provided by their employers. In the yard there is then likely to be a range of traditional buildings that are no longer practical for current farming methods and lie empty.

On the land as well the emphasis has changed, with smaller or steeper fields being too cumbersome to cultivate, or with problems arising where the farm borders a town or village. These factors are of course only too well known to the incumbent farmer who literally lives with them and must ask himself frequently whether better use could not be made of them. He is therefore perhaps well placed to identify an alternative potential within some part of his own property.

At this initial stage, one would expect just to devise some alternative use and be confident in being able to adapt the land or buildings accordingly. After all, such change has been managed successfully by farmers for hundreds of years: the threshing floor in the tithe barn would have given way to storage bins; the old cowshed will have been converted to calf pens; and the more difficult headlands perhaps taken out of cultivation and planted with trees for sporting cover. Today, however, things have become more regulated and one cannot always rely solely upon one's own ingenuity. Having therefore identified a new use for a part of the farm and established that it could be feasible from the financial and managerial aspects, one should also be aware of the kind of practical issues that will need to be investigated further.

3.3.1 The buildings

Making new use of an old range of buildings is one of the most common forms of farm diversification and would therefore seem to be the most straightforward, but will none the less incur the kind of wider issues raised just mentioned. A building conversion is likely to attract a greater movement of vehicles than in its present probably semi-redundant state and would form part of the considerations when planning consent is applied for. The authorities will need to be satisfied that the existing access on to the public road is adequate and can properly fulfil modern requirements. If not, then an alternative solution might be to construct a new access elsewhere, that will have a wider approach and better sightlines on to the road, but this will involve an extra cost that would not have been anticipated when the scheme was first devised. Such an alternative might of course not be available or the public road itself be deemed too narrow or too populated for such extra traffic to be permitted. These matters are described more fully in chapter 8, but are introduced here to illustrate the range of issues that may need to be considered when deciding to make a change to an existing building. Another important consideration is that of Building Regulations, which will need to be adhered to when gaining planning consent and which can impose certain compulsory requirements on crucial features such as headroom or ventilation. The old farm buildings would have been constructed to quite different specifications to those considered necessary for human accommodation today and in many cases it will be impossible now to adapt them accordingly.

One initial idea about putting old buildings to a new use can therefore give rise to a wide range of further issues that will need to be resolved. It is important at the outset to be aware of these and to consider whether they might have to be investigated in more detail as part of the initial appraisal. It is one thing to have, like our forebears, the imagination and the practical ability to adapt a building to a new use, but today one needs as well to be able to recognise the possible impact of current regulatory requirement.

3.3.2 *The land*

Where land is being taken out of an existing farming business to be used for another purpose, the resulting loss to the original business must be accounted for. This may involve wider considerations than the financial consequences that were mentioned earlier in section 3.1.1. For example, if the land is registered under the Integrated Administration and Control System (IACS) or has milk quota allocated against it, then arrangements should be made to ensure as far as possible that these valuable attributes are not be lost, but swapped or transferred to another area.

One needs to check that the land is well enough suited to its new purpose. If it were planned to use former arable headlands as the route for horse riding, one would have to avoid wet or heavy areas that might become badly damaged under the new usage and could then operate only during a limited period. Land classification can be significant too. Although most farmers would try to avoid taking their better land out of agricultural production, if that land is classified as Grade 1 or 2 it could be more difficult to gain planning consent. Where the new venture involves building work as well as a change in land use, one may overlook initially the fact that there may be costs in converting the land as well as the buildings, such as drainage or fencing or reseeding.

3.3.3 *Location*

Location is always a crucial element in any property matter. In planning a change of use this can be particularly true, but it is a matter that can be easily overlooked by someone who has lived and worked on the farm for years and has become quite accustomed to its situation. The full implications of this are discussed in section 10.2, but at this stage it is worth just checking whether the position of the property is likely to help or hinder the proposed new venture. The constraints of running commercial traffic down rural lanes have already been mentioned in section 3.3.1 above. Other enterprises may involve only light traffic, such as a bed and breakfast business, but if it is located in a little visited part of the country or at some distance from a main road, it might be difficult to attract a sufficient number of guests. Even an agricultural diversification scheme, such as one involving a new form of crop or livestock, may be affected by being in a remote location if it were dependent on making deliveries to a processing plant or alternatively to direct selling to the public.

3.4 Planning permission

Introducing a new venture on to a farm will tend to require planning consent, especially where it involves building development or a significant change of use. The planning process is discussed in chapter 8 but the basic issues need to be considered at an early stage in order to establish whether the proposed diversification would be permitted or not and whether particular conditions might be imposed.

In most cases, one will not be able to establish for certain that planning consent will be forthcoming without making a formal application, which will require detailed work and therefore time, and expense. However, there are ways in which one can gain some indication on this without going to such formal lengths. First, one might refer to the Structure and Local Plans, which are available at council offices and libraries. These plans set out current planning policy within the district. They define the locations that have been designated for certain types of developments or other activities and also the remaining areas in which no particular change is envisaged. If one's property lies outside one of the designated zones, then it may be assumed that any development would have to be considered on the strength of its own merit rather than on fulfilling the aims of current policy. A further indication might then be gained by discussing the proposal informally with a planning officer at the council. While such discussions cannot provide any firm indication that permission would be granted, they may establish the aspects on which the council would need to be satisfied.

It may well be that professional help will be needed in preparing a planning application, from an architect, planning consultant or chartered surveyor, and there might therefore be opportunity to discuss the situation with such an adviser at this initial stage. It should then be possible to gain a view as to the likelihood of planning consent being granted and the extent of any extra work that might be required as a condition of such permission being given. At the same time, where constructional alterations are going to be made, one could establish whether there would be any particular prohibitions or requirements under the Building Regulations or for the Highway Authority.

3.5 Market appraisal

This seemingly innocuous sounding title covers what can be the most vital, and most difficult, function in planning a new venture. One needs to establish whether there will be enough demand for whatever product is being planned, the reliability of such demand during the foreseeable future and the price that it could currently command. This may be a matter of just applying some standard price to the product and multiplying it by the assumed output but it could also require a more sophisticated analysis of the local and national market and assessing other existing suppliers, the quality of their goods and the price that their customers appear to be willing to pay. Either way, one must try to assess as realistically as possible the potential net income over the first few years together with any possible constraints or opportunities.

3.6 Management and personnel

It has already been mentioned that most new enterprises are instigated by financial or physical reasons. In other words, there will either have been a need to improve income or a chance to exploit a potential market, or an opportunity to make better use of a building or of some area of land. It is therefore these factors that tend to be considered first, as outlined in the preceding sections, but it is important also to check whether there will be the necessary skills and management resources to run the new venture. It is one thing to identify a project and to devise plans and budgets for it but it may be another matter then to run it successfully, particularly when it is something that has no bearing on previous farming experience. At this stage, it is therefore worth assessing whether the existing personnel would be likely to have the time and ability to undertake both the management and the labouring tasks or whether some training or outside assistance should be allowed for.

3.7 Timing

Before embarking upon a new development it is worth trying to work out how long it might take to complete, especially if where it may have a seasonal element like a facility for tourists or a new crop. One would want to avoid a situation in which all the planning and building work was being done during the season and completed at the start of a winter lull. In this situation there would be a delay until the following spring before the venture started to earn any income. In the meantime the development costs would have been carried in full. It might even be better to postpone the start of a newly designed scheme if it meant that there would be less delay before it began earning income.

3.8 Conclusion

These various considerations are in many ways interdependent and the order in which one would be best advised to investigate them will be determined by the circumstances. At this initial stage, it should become clear which facets are going to be the most crucial or likely to be the more difficult to resolve and which are less significant. Where it becomes apparent that a specific issue may give rise to such difficulties, then it may be that this will need to be investigated in more detail early on before continuing with a wider appraisal. It is important therefore at the very outset to have checked through all the possible features so as to establish everything that will need to be done. This will avoid the danger of unexpected problems arising at a later stage when they could cause difficulties or delays and even result in abortive costs. By taking such a broad initial approach, it is possible that one might also identify some additional potential to the original scheme that had not been thought of before and would now warrant further attention.

3.9 Check-list

- Where a new venture means replacing part of the existing business, be aware of the resulting loss of income, facilities, and employment. Balance against this however the benefits of reduced costs and of sale proceeds of stock and equipment.
- Check how proposals such as building plans might impact on the value of the property as a whole, whether adversely or positively.
- Prepare an outline budget for the venture, based on estimates of income, overheads and establishment costs. Estimate the time scale for when income would be received and how reliable it might be.
- Make initial enquiries as to raising finance, whether as an extension of existing facilities or from new sources.
- Find out what planning and building regulations would need to be observed and identify potential problem areas.
- Check designations, both as to environmental controls and those relating to agricultural subsidies and production.
- Carry out preliminary market research, regarding the product and also the suitability of both the property and the people that are to be involved.

3.9.1 *Sources of advice and information*

- Bank account manager
- Accountant

- Land agent
- Trade organisations and individuals already engaged in that type of enterprise
- Local planning authority
- Rural Property Database

Chapter Four

Identifying the Opportunities

The initial analysis referred to in the previous chapter introduces a whole range of issues that are likely to arise with diversification and which will need to be considered in more detail at some later stage. Before doing so, however, it would be worth carrying out a simple appraisal of one's own situation as a means of discovering where such opportunities might be found. This would be essentially a review of all the main features of the property and of the existing business as well as one's personal circumstances and can be done by taking a logical look at each aspect in turn.

4.1 The premises

4.1.1 The buildings

Farm buildings represent a valuable asset, if only because to construct them today would involve prohibitive costs and potential resistance from the planning authorities. However some may be outdated and of seemingly little benefit to the farm and there are a number of questions that one should ask:

Are all the buildings being used or might there be some that are not really needed for the present day farm business? So often there may be an old barn that cannot be entered by modern machinery and has therefore become a repository for all sorts of items, many of which are no longer worth keeping or could easily be stored elsewhere. It could therefore readily be vacated and made available for some other purpose. Where such an opportunity exists it should certainly be considered as a potential for some form of diversification. It may be that this would then prove to be unfeasible due perhaps to its location in the middle of the yard or to its poor condition. It is none the less important to have identified the possibility and then checked whether it would be likely to convert to a new purpose.

Even if all the buildings are in use, are they being profitable? Given the recent plight of the beef sector, there could well be situations in which a covered yard is still used for cattle even though the herd has been making a loss each year. Unless one can foresee an improvement in the market, logic would dictate that the stock should be sold with the consequence that the building would become vacant. In practice, of course, the decision may be more difficult to make; there may have been a tradition of having cattle on the farm that is not easily abandoned, or a need for farmyard manure to support an organic enterprise, or prices may be so low that it would seem better to retain the herd for the time being despite the losses. It can be difficult too to see any alternative for such buildings when they are deep in straw and manure and draughty and unlit. Yet there could well be a commercial alternative once it was cleaned and perhaps re-clad. Barn conversions are no longer confined just to picturesque traditional buildings but are also being applied increasingly to more modern portal framed structures as well.

Then, if all the buildings are not only in use but are also accommodating a profitable enterprise, are they in fact well enough suited for that purpose? It may be that one could find that they were more valuable for some alternative use and that it would be worth transferring the existing farm activity to other premises. It may no longer be necessary to put up with the inconvenience of working around internal stanchions or mucking out by hand, if that building could be successfully converted to another purpose. The funds raised thereby could go towards providing, for example, a lean-to elsewhere that could then be adapted to provide appropriate accommodation for the calf pens, the workshop or whatever function the older premises had still been used for.

Buildings seem to be such a permanent feature of a farmyard that it can be difficult to see them as an adaptable asset and yet increasingly they can be the key to unlocking a substantial new opportunity whether as an income earning enterprise or as a capital development. It is important therefore to be able to look beyond the current arrangements and to identify such possible opportunities. One must be careful, however, not to assume that every practical inconvenience can be resolved by this means or that even the most attractive of old barns will have development potential. The physical and financial constraints already alluded to in chapter 3 must be recognised too, but it will always be useful to have assessed how well the buildings are being used at present and to have considered at least what the other possibilities might be.

4.1.2 Cottages

It is well known that agriculture used to employ a far larger number of people than today and that, due to the long hours and a lack of mobility, such workers were accommodated on the property. Many farms still have cottages that would have been erected for this purpose. Now there may no longer be any employees at all or those few that do work on the land will have their own cars and will have chosen to live in a nearby village. As a result there could well be cottages that are surplus to the requirements of the business and which should perhaps be put to another use. In many cases they may already have been sold or let on residential tenancies. In some areas, these cottages now represent an almost disproportionate value, whether as a possible sale or in terms of a residential rent or holiday letting.

This potential may seem readily apparent, but there may be a number of further considerations that will also need to be assessed. Even if cottages are no longer required by the farm business, their disposal could adversely affect the value of the remaining property if it were to reduce the privacy of the main house. As farming is changing so rapidly, it could be that such accommodation would again be needed in conjunction with some new specialised venture, rather than just to house a wage earner. Traditionally, these cottages are more old fashioned than housing in other areas. There may be a case for investing in some improvements before offering them for sale or to let. On the other hand, being of a traditional nature, they can often involve the owner in ongoing maintenance costs, which could be avoided in future depending on the means of disposal.

Often too, cottages are being occupied by former employees on an arrangement for life and the owners may assume that they cannot in all conscience suggest that they be moved. It could be, however, that as the occupants become more elderly they would welcome less isolated accommodation and would be happy to move into a village. This might then be arranged, even with the help of the local housing authority if it meant that it were to lead to more economic activity in the area through holiday lettings or some other diversification scheme. Many dwellings that were constructed on farms during the last 50 years will be subject to a planning restriction requiring them to be used only by persons engaged in agriculture. This would appear to exclude their availability for other residential or diversified purposes and in many cases this will be so. There are however legitimate means whereby such restrictions can be removed and one should not therefore dismiss the possibility that such cottages might be used for a non-farming enterprise.

The initial overview should therefore register the current use and condition of the cottages and identify how their removal or alteration might affect the farm as a whole. There may be potential for increasing income and reducing overheads or for raising capital. However there could also be a danger that one would thereby erode the longer term values of the whole.

4.1.3 *The farmhouse*

The farmhouse can be the single most valuable asset on the whole property and, while there is a tendency for farms to be amalgamated and for their former houses to command high residential values, there could well be potential for selling or letting them separately. These houses are, however, more than just a business asset being not only a family home but also the very heart of the enterprise. Decisions affecting the house are therefore difficult to make, but they must none the less be included within the appraisal.

Despite the high values prevailing in certain areas, it will not just be a question of whether to sell or let, although this might in fact be a realistic option where an alternative home could be found on the farm such as in one of the cottages. None the less, farmhouses are often larger than other equivalent country homes, having been built to accommodate several generations living and working together. This is now increasingly noticeable as fewer younger people remain on the land and as the average age of farmers rises accordingly. For example, there could well be spare space that could be used for bed and breakfast accommodation. This needs not only to be identified but also to be assessed in terms of how readily it could be incorporated within the house and how much it would impinge on the rest of the accommodation.

A farmhouse may well be the family home but it also often includes a room that is used as the farm office. If a new business is being introduced, it is likely that such an arrangement would no longer be adequate with there then being a greater amount of administration and with perhaps outside personnel being involved as well. It might become necessary to find an alternative location for the office, possibly within the farmyard or as part of a new development, leaving the house free of commercial activity.

There have been cases in the past where it has been accepted that the main house is no longer appropriate to a working farm, due to its size, style or value and that permission has been granted for a more suitable one to be built elsewhere on the land. The original premises would then be sold as a private residence. While this is not strictly speaking a form of diversification, it should no doubt be borne in mind when assessing the overall circumstances.

4.1.4 *Situation*

When assessing whether these premises could be better used than at present, one must also check whether their situation is suited to such possibilities. Do the buildings have an adequate access to allow them to be used for a non-agricultural purpose? Can they be separated from the main farmstead, if needed? Would they be adversely affected by the continuing farming activities, such as noise from machinery or mess from livestock? Similarly, is there a danger that the proposed activities within the buildings might impinge upon the working and the enjoyment of the house and farm?

Cottages too are often sited beside the farmstead and their residential potential might be hampered by the noise and smell of the farm. Similar considerations can apply to the main house as well, if it is close to the yard and is to be occupied separately from the farm.

4.1.5 *Condition*

The public is inclined to have a picturesque image of the countryside and could easily be disappointed by the reality of many working farmyards, where things can become weedy, muddy and cluttered with old machinery and items of apparent rubbish. If part of the property is to be occupied by outsiders, one will have to check that there are both the resources and the inclination to keep the yard and buildings and the adjacent land in suitable order.

4.2 The land

One should ask oneself whether the present farm business is dependent upon using all the land on the property and whether there are any areas that are either not that well suited to agriculture or that could be given up without significant loss. There are often certain fields that are more difficult to cultivate than others and somehow fate has a way of placing these areas in full public view so that everyone sees the worst of one's crops! If that really were to be the case, then the chances are that these areas will be near a road and therefore accessible and potentially suitable for other uses.

It may be that an idea has already been formulated for a scheme that would require the use of some of the land that is currently being used by the farm, whether for a caravan site or for biomass production or some other non-agricultural venture. One needs then to check what the consequences would be on the farm business if its area of operations were reduced by the acreage that would be taken by the new enterprise. It would also be worth seeing whether the land earmarked for this purpose were to be of a particular value to the farm or whether it would be better to try and select another site on the property that comprised an area of lesser agricultural quality. Such matters as IACS registration and permanent setaside will also need to be taken into account as well as the question of the economic efficiency of the reduced farm business.

In selecting such a site one must be sure that it is well enough suited to that purpose, not only in being separately accessed if need be but also in its physical characteristics. One may be encouraged to take the poorest land and so cause the least loss to the farm, but that may then not be good enough even for the new venture. For example, land that lies wet may not be conducive to easy arable cultivation but it will also be a problem for many other activities whether horse riding or car boot sales or even as grazing by exotic livestock. How crucial these limitations might be may depend on the length of season for which the land would be required. If a caravan site is being planned on the basis that as it is close to the coast it will only be operated in the summer, then it may be possible to use a location such as a river meadow. Indeed, this might be particularly advantageous as it would be an attractive position and therefore more readily sought after by the visiting public. If however the whole venture depends upon being open throughout a longer season then a site that might lie wet or even flood in the spring or autumn would have to be discounted.

4.3 Location

Location is a fundamental consideration in almost every diversification scheme and one which might rather be taken for granted due to the fact that each individual situation has become so familiar over the years in which the farmer may have lived and worked there. It is clear however that a rural business venture that succeeds in one part of the country might not work at all in a different sort of area. It is important at the outset to analyse the particular features of the locality in which the property is situated.

What sort of area is it? Is it mainly agricultural or are there other interests there as well? If so, do the non-farming communities live there and work locally or commute? Is it frequented by visitors and do they come on a daily basis or for weekends or on holidays? What sort of image does the neighbourhood have; is it a pretty, and therefore probably protected countryside, or more workaday? Has there been much new development? Does this imply a proactive local planning policy that would favour further schemes or is there then a danger that too many would be allowed and that there could then be excessive competition? Within this scenario, does the farm itself have features that could be exploited such an old fashioned yard that would be attractive to visitors in a tourist area? Alternatively, does it only have a modern range of buildings that are neither attractive nor readily convertible to anything but commercial uses?

In recognising the nature of the locality one can assess more clearly the kind of operations that would be likely to attract demand as well as those that would be unsuitable. One can weigh up also what sort of ventures might already be oversubscribed and which others might be acceptable to the local planning authority. This assessment should also consider any changes that are occurring within the area and therefore anticipate opportunities that seem likely to arise in the future.

4.4 Human resources

Human resources is an expression more readily associated with multi-national corporations than family farms, but it does none the less describe quite well an important aspect of rural diversification. The property may be found to be well suited for a particular form of new business, due to its layout or location, but this can only be successfully developed if the people that are to be involved are well suited to it as well. This has already been mentioned in section 3.6; if the project is to be run by the farmer or his wife or by someone currently working on the farm, one should just make sure that they are ready and able to undertake this new role. Developing and then managing a new venture will demand both time and energy, especially at the outset. It is important to assess whether it will be possible to do all this while still continuing with the farm business. It may be that the farm has been reduced in some way so as to enable the diversification to take place, but the working time that would thereby be saved might easily be less than that required by the new enterprise. If it is likely then that extra help will be needed on the farm at certain times and the implications of using contractors should be considered, in terms not only of costs but also of the overall standard of management. The different seasonal demands on the farm should of course be considered against the labour requirements of the new business; providing holiday accommodation, for example, will be at its most busy just at the time when the cereal harvest is under way. This would mean not only that additional help would be required possibly for both sides of the business, but that it is likely also to be more stressful. Offering the same accommodation on an autumn calving dairy farm, on the other hand, would probably be more easily managed.

Where the venture is going to be run by someone from outside one needs to be sure that such a person would fit in with the existing arrangements. It can be difficult on both sides when a newcomer is introduced into what is often the rather traditional environment of a farm business. This is especially true at a time when agriculture is already suffering losses and when the new venture is under pressure to perform.

4.5 Finance

It is also worth taking stock of the actual financial situation. How urgent is the need to introduce a new source of income? If the farm is already making losses that need to be rectified quickly then one may have to take a more determined and courageous view of the various diversification options, knowing that one cannot afford too much delay. On the other hand, if the financial position is still sound one might allow a little extra time to assess the full implications of the proposed scheme and to weigh up carefully one's motives and rationale for embarking upon it in the first place. Preparing a new project of this kind usually demands a high degree of initiative and enthusiasm and it is not always easy then to find the right opportunity to balance this against all those more conservative issues that also need to be taken into account.

Furthermore, how difficult might it be to raise the necessary finance and from whom? The various options are considered in chapter 5, but at this stage one should weigh up the overall financial position of the farm and the likely attitude of the bank, both individually at a local level and as according to prevailing policies throughout the rural sector. It is important too to assess how this position might change and what risk there might be that bank support could be reduced or withdrawn prematurely due to a change in attitude in the future. If funding is to be obtained from other available sources such as the family or private investors, the full implications of becoming beholden to them should be considered. The cost of finance is also an issue that will need to be estimated at some stage.

4.6 The market

The question of timing and of the pace at which the project should be developed has also to be considered in the context of the market in which the new venture will be operating. In certain situations it may be necessary to press on as soon as possible, as in the case of a seasonal business such as one depending on summer visitors or where there is a possibility that someone else within the locality may be planning a similar venture that would take away part of the potential demand. Otherwise, there may always be an advantage in taking time just to review the whole situation, both in the context of the specifics mentioned above and overall as discussed in section 4.9 below.

4.7 Local feeling

By this stage these various deliberations may well have brought one to the conclusion that it would be right to proceed with the proposed diversification and that there would be a number of advantages in doing so. Not only might it be fulfilling some essential commercial function such as providing additional income or longer term security and continuity for the family farm, but it could also be providing a new service or attraction for visitors and residents alike, as well as creating some local employment. Such apparent advantages will not however ensure that everyone in the neighbourhood would necessarily welcome the proposals.

The countryside is a traditional place and many people within it, especially those not directly connected with farming, can be strongly resistant to any innovation or change. These views may not always seem realistic or reasonable to the long established and now hard pressed farmer. One's inclination might be to ignore them and to press on regardless. Local opinion can however be a crucial issue, especially when seeking planning permission, as mentioned in chapter 8. It will be as well to weigh up what the likely reaction of people within the locality would be to the proposed scheme. This would be not just for the sake of securing agreement to the planning application, but also because rural enterprises do often depend upon being accepted and supported by the local community. So many diversification schemes involve contact with the public, whether they are commercial tenants or shop customers or holiday makers. One cannot run the risk of having to maintain a business relationship with them in an atmosphere of antagonism. If people within the immediate area are unhappy about these new activities, those involved in them could suffer endless inconvenience. This might be in the form of complaints about noise and traffic or by having a poor reputation broadcast around or by showing an unhelpful attitude to visitors when stopping to ask the way. An important part of one's overall appraisal will therefore be to assess the feelings of the local community and to judge how serious any opposition might be and what steps might have to be taken to overcome it.

4.8 Tenants

Even though they do not own or control their farms, tenants can still have the same range of opportunities for diversification as owner-occupiers and should therefore go through the same appraisal process. If a proposed scheme appears to be feasible and seems unlikely also to prejudice the long term integrity of the farm, the landlord might be expected to give consent to a tenant's proposal to change the use of part of the holding. It is possible too that the landlord could provide all or part of the finance needed or enter into a joint venture arrangement. Furthermore, by having to put the matter before the managing agent the tenant would benefit from getting a professional response to the suggested venture.

Alternatively, by making a thorough assessment of the farm, a tenant might identify land or buildings that could be released for another purpose in the same way as in section 4.1.1 above. Some agreement might then be reached whereby these areas could be relinquished from the lease so as to allow the landlord to develop some non-agricultural use. This can be of mutual advantage in circumstances where it might be difficult for the tenant to raise the necessary capital while the landlord has access to funds for implementing the project, either from his own resources or in partnership with another party such as a developer. The tenant would thereby gain a rent reduction and possibly be freed from the obligation to continue to maintain outdated buildings. In coming to such agreement, the tenant should however try to ensure that any new development would be carried out in such a manner as not to disturb his continued occupation of the rest of the holding.

4.9 Overview

The approach taken so far has been to recognise the current state of the business, assess the various factors involved and identify new opportunities that may provide added income or capital value. In many cases, the next step to be made will require a growing degree of commitment, in time and money, as well as in personal involvement and even inconvenience. Before proceeding, it would therefore be prudent to review the overall situation.

Two of the main premises on which diversification is based are:

- a need to rectify falling income, at a time of continuing decline
- exploiting the many new opportunities occurring in the countryside

It is worth taking a view as to how these two scenarios may change in the foreseeable future. Most diversification schemes involve a significant amount of both time and money before they are likely to show a positive return and they also incur a varying degree of risk. One needs therefore to be reasonably sure that market conditions are unlikely to change significantly for the worse, at least for the time required until the venture has been able to show a proper return on the initial investment. It is not easy to predict such things, especially when breaking new ground as is so often the case with diversification, and there is tendency anyway to assume somehow that today's conditions will last forever. One needs only to look at statistical graphs to see how markets are always changing.

Interest rates, that can be the root of a major cost in diversification schemes, provide one such example. Latterly we have become

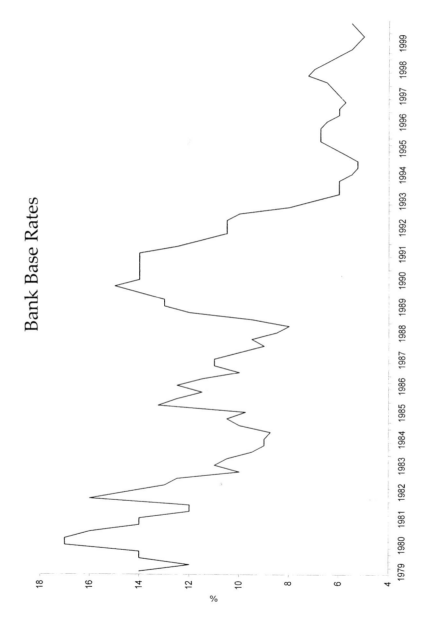

Bank Base Rates

Source: Bank of England

accustomed to relatively low interest rates and may no longer plan for the possibility that interest charges could again become a heavy burden. Yet in Figure 1, which shows the movement over the last 20 years of bank base rate, we can see a dramatic pattern of peaks and troughs and are reminded of a time when interest charges were over three times their present level. Taking this one particular example further, one would be prompted to ask two questions: will interest rates fluctuate again to those earlier levels and what would therefore now be the best type of loan to take out? To answer the first, one may be tempted to assume that history tends to repeat itself and that one should therefore be prepared to face higher rates during the period of a loan that might be for 10 or 15 years. On the other hand, many financial experts would point out that things have been irrevocably altered through the introduction of the Euro and that there is every reason to expect rates to remain relatively low for evermore. Either way, the second question would lead to a consideration of the possible advantage of arranging all or part of one's finance on a fixed term basis. That would then protect the business against the uncertainty of future fluctuations. If the markets are generally of the view that rates will remain more stable, such fixed loans would be relatively cheap and the decision might therefore be more easily made.

Another crucial case would be that of farm incomes that have, on average, been in decline over the last few years. This may well have been the prime cause of prompting many people to take the initiative to diversify, as it offers a means of trading one's way out of what would appear to be an inescapable shortfall. In this instance, happily, many commentators believe that the graph will rise again shortly and that incomes will recover. If that did happen soon enough and to a sufficient degree, there might never have been the need to undertake the difficult and uncertain process of diversification. It would again have been wise to have looked carefully at this whole issue before embarking upon an enterprise solely in order to counter the prevailing deterioration of agricultural incomes. It is possible of course that, having taken a view on such a matter, one would still decide to proceed for a number of possible reasons: that one is not sufficiently confident of those experts' predictions; or that there could be a further downturn in later years; or that the trends suggest that whatever recovery there may be to average incomes there would still be problems for farms of a certain size or type; and that diversification will yet have to be the answer. In reaching this conclusion one will however at least have the reassurance of doing so with the benefit of having weighed up the various options before going ahead.

Meanwhile, the future success of the new venture needs to be considered in the same way as the outlook for farming. There is always the danger that the market on which it is dependent will weaken, due to becoming oversubscribed or to losing popularity, especially if it is, as so often, breaking into new and relatively untested areas. This is dealt with further in chapter 7 on marketing. At this preliminary stage it is certainly worth trying to identify the main issues that are likely to affect the commercial success of the new venture and to foresee how they could change over the coming years.

The purpose of this initial overview seems to be largely negative, suggesting that new enterprises are difficult and risky to establish and that one should exercise great care and caution before going ahead. In so many instances this is indeed be the case and it would be only sensible then to have taken proper note of the relevant warning signs. There can however also be more positive aspects which it would be equally important to recognise and which can be useful in providing one with the right encouragement when embarking upon a venture that might otherwise seem rather daunting or dangerous. These may arise from local circumstances, such as when there is a gap in a market that can be seen to work well elsewhere, or also from national or political factors. For example, current Government policy on both planning and the economy seem likely to bring more development to some rural areas and to channel financial support into others. These wider issues can be just as important when appraising the future of a new enterprise as the more specific factors concerning the particular property or people involved.

There are of course no definite answers either to the future of the various agricultural sectors or to the outlook for new enterprises. However it would be as well at least to identify the key areas upon which the viability of the proposed scheme would depend and to gain an informed view as to how they are likely to develop in the coming years. One needs also to be realistic about the performance of the current farming business and the way in which it is likely to be affected by future market changes. If there are doubts about its continued viability, then some changes will have to be introduced. These may, however, not necessarily be in the form of a new non-farming enterprise if the general circumstances are unfavourable. Just because diversification is the current trend and there seem to be many examples of successful schemes being established around the country does not imply that it will be the answer in every situation. Not only must the circumstances be well suited to the proposed venture, but the individual's aptitude and ability will be a major factor. It may well be that present business performance needs to be enhanced and that there are opportunities available for diversification, but that the soundest solution will still be to find solutions within the agricultural field, such as by restructuring with contractors or tenants.

4.10 Checklist

- Take stock of all the basic business factors:

Buildings:	their current use, suitability for that use and potential for alternatives
Cottages:	how currently occupied; whether still required and whether changes might be made
Farmhouse:	whether still best suited as a family home or whether some of the accommodation could be put to commercial use
The land:	whether all being best used for farming and if part could easily be released for another purpose
Location:	what are the main features of the area, especially in terms of non-agricultural communities and activity
Management:	whether the individuals involved would have the time, ability and aptitude to raise the necessary capital
Finance:	the need to create additional income and the ability to raise capital
Attitudes:	what resistance there might be from local people and how best this might be overcome

- Tenants to discuss possibilities with Landlord.
- Take a wider view of present trends and how future events might impact upon one's plans and on the present business.
- Take stock of current income, the need for improvement and whether it would be best achieved by diversification or through other restructuring.

4.10.1 *Sources of advice and information*

- Accountant
- Land agent or farming consultant
- Local planning office
- Local chamber of commerce

Chapter Five

Finance

5.1 Capital

In most instances, starting a new venture will involve a capital outlay. This may be only a minor amount, as in such cases when farm labour might be used to convert old calf pens into stables. It can also be quite substantial if, for example, a complete new building is to be erected by contractors. In principle, raising finance for diversification is little different to funding any normal farming requirement, although there may be a number of additional features to consider.

An inexpensive scheme may be funded from past years' profits or perhaps from cash reserves. This will then just be a matter of deciding whether those resources are best used for the planned diversification or whether they might yet be needed elsewhere. If existing capital is being used, allowance should be made for the fact that one will be foregoing the return that it will have been showing until now, whether that was in the form of interest or dividends. The income that has been foregone can also have been from a more direct source such as when a dairy herd and quota is sold in order to raise capital. Either way, there will be a reduction in current income that will effectively be the cost of funding the new work from one's own resources. More often, however, the cost of establishing the new venture will need to be financed from outside sources.

5.1.1 Capital cost

Before exploring in any detail the source of finance, it will be necessary to establish the likely cost of the venture. An initial estimate may well have been made along the lines explained in section 3.2. This will, at some stage, need to be worked in more detail particularly if an approach is to be made for funds from an outside party such as a bank. Where building works are going to be involved, the likely cost can probably be assessed by a surveyor or architect, which will then be substantiated at a later stage in the tenders submitted by contractors. One should be careful to include all the costs that are going to arise as well as just those of actually doing the new building works. These might include, for example, the demolition of an existing barn or shed or the planting of a screen of young trees. Also, where construction equipment is being brought on to a farm it may be necessary to raise or remove temporarily electric power lines and culverts may have to be strengthened or gateways widened. Not all of these further costs will be of great significance in themselves but it is as well to have arrived at a reasonable total figure at the start rather than find later that one has under-estimated the cost and not made sufficient financial provision to complete the project.

Work that is to be carried out by farm labour may not have to be costed into the estimates if their time is genuinely available, but one should check whether this is likely to have any impact on the existing business. Some other tasks may not be carried out as well as before due to the demands of working on the diversification scheme and there could be an increased amount of overtime to be paid. On arable farms it may have been reckoned that there would be capacity to do this work in the winter time when farm duties are lighter than in the growing or harvesting seasons. It is possible that the whole project will have been delayed by any number of factors, such as gaining planning consent or waiting for contractors to complete an essential task, so that the work will have to be done at an unforeseen time when everyone on the farm is busy.

5.1.2 Borrowings

Where the capital is to be found from borrowings, the cost is more directly identifiable and a number of choices need to be made.

Other than for the smaller schemes where the required capital might be obtainable through an extension of existing overdraft facilities, the necessary funds would normally be raised through a loan. This may be either secured or unsecured, the former being sometimes easier to arrange and possibly at a slightly lower rate of interest, while the latter carries a lesser risk. The actual type of loan taken may well be determined by the particular terms being offered by one's bank or by a specialist lender such as the Agricultural Mortgage Corporation. It is not the purpose of this book to consider all the various arrangements that might be available. A list of some of the principal sources of finance is however given in the Appendix and there are some general principles that will need to be considered in all cases. These are discussed below.

The first issue that normally comes to mind when taking out a loan is the cost of the interest. This will raise some standard questions as to the prevailing rates of interest, whether they will be fixed or variable, on what frequency the payments are to be made and whether these are to include an element of capital repayment or be on an interest only basis. As the loan is to be for a new venture, there will be a further question as to how the initial interest payments are to be met. The capital is likely to be required at the outset in order to fund building works and other costs, but the enterprise itself may take some while before it is sufficiently developed to produce a proper income flow. Arrangements will therefore have to be made to cover the interest charges in the meantime. This may be by drawing upon income from the existing farm business, or by agreeing with the lender that interest becomes payable only after a certain time, or possibly by taking out a slightly larger loan than the actual capital amount required and using the surplus to pay off the first interest payments as they become due. In any event, allowance will have to be made for this, whether merely by accounting properly for the temporary reduction in farm income or by negotiating the right terms under which the loan is to be taken out.

The rate of interest on a loan being taken out to start a new venture could differ from that applied to any borrowings that might already be in place on the farm. This reflects the greater risk and uncertainty of starting what is probably an untried enterprise compared to running a well established farm and one must not therefore assume that a bank will necessarily make funds available on the same terms as those already offered. It could also be that there will be some constraints as to the period over which the loan is to be repaid. Agriculture is recognised as a long term business that generally shows only modest returns, but which is well secured against the value of the land. As a result mortgages tend to be for relatively long periods, such as 20 or 25 years. However, in the case of a non-farming scheme there will be less evidence about its reliability and greater uncertainty as to its future, but with possibly a greater potential to show a higher return in a shorter period. This means that lenders may seek to limit the period over which they are committed to an involvement in the project and might also expect it to be able to produce better returns and so repay the loan and interest in a shorter time.

The terms of a loan are determined also in part by the commercial standing of the borrower, but diversification may often be planned by another party such as the farmer's wife or son. This might mean again that one should be prepared for a slightly higher rate of interest than that being charged on existing loans. It may be that this will be mitigated by the farmer or someone with a recognised track record or collateral being asked to act as guarantor. The implications of this are dealt with briefly in the section on legal issues in chapter 9.

In any event, when seeking a loan for a new and untried venture the lender may need to be reassured as to the viability of the scheme and the ability of the borrower to develop it successfully. Even where the borrower may already have an account or a loan agreement for the existing farm business with a financial institution, a proper case would still have to be made for the new arrangement, involving, for example, well worked budgets and evidence of market research.

A secured loan, such as a mortgage, is assessed not only on the ability of the borrower to pay the interest charges, but also on the value of the property against which it is secured. If the farm already has a mortgage and this is to be increased to provide the necessary funds for diversification, then the new total amount borrowed will have to be within a prescribed percentage of the value of the property. In those cases where the existing mortgage is already up to the maximum percentage allowed by that lender, the additional amount may yet be granted if it can be shown that the value of the farm will be enhanced by the development of the proposed new enterprise. One would assume that this further investment will result in an improved value of the whole property, although there have been instances where sadly this has not been so, such as with some conversions of farmland into golf courses. Even when the new development does itself have a positive value, this could be offset to some extent by the effect that it might have on the remaining property. For example, a period farmhouse that is situated next to some traditional barns may provide an attractive residential setting and command a high value. This could however be seriously impaired if the barns were divided off and converted to commercial use. It may also be in an agricultural recession and falling land market, when there can be a greater incentive to consider diversification, that the asset value has decreased and that the lenders are beginning to take a more cautious line and are requiring a greater degree of collateral cover. It would be as well then to check the value of the property as a whole before assuming that, just because the projected income is capable of servicing the interest, a new mortgage will be granted or an existing one extended.

Where a lender appears wary of lending against a new venture, it may be feasible to raise the loan against the assets and business of the existing farm alone even though the funds are due to be used for an alternative purpose. It must be remembered that there is a risk associated with taking out a mortgage. If for whatever reason the borrower were to default on the payments as they become due, then the lender would be entitled to sell the property in order to recoup any outstanding sums. Happily, this has occurred only very rarely in farming but embarking on a new non-agricultural venture can involve a greater degree of uncertainty and this must be recognised before deciding to use the main farm as collateral for finance.

There appear then to be a number of potential disadvantages when seeking loan finance for a diversification project as opposed to that available for the normal farm business. This can create a tendency to try to develop the scheme within existing borrowing facilities, such as the overdraft. That can however inevitably lead to problems at a later stage, by which time it could be crucial to have reliable and ongoing support from one's bank. If the proposed scheme has been properly researched and can therefore be shown to be likely to succeed, then one should be able to negotiate satisfactory terms for its funding. Much of this will depend upon the anticipated income, which is considered further in section 5.2 below.

It may be that the project can be financed in part by one's own capital and that the borrowings will be needed only be for the remaining portion of the total cost. This can be an advantage when negotiating terms with a lender who will have a lesser exposure to the scheme as a whole and may be encouraged by the fact that the borrower is making a personal commitment to it as well.

5.1.3 Investors

The capital needed to develop a proposed diversification can also be sourced from an outside investor. This is likely to be some person or organisation that would have a direct interest in the type of business or market in which the scheme is involved. It would probably be on the basis of a partnership or co-operation whereby the farmer would provide one part of the equity in the form of the original property and the investor would contribute the funds needed to implement the scheme. The farmer or landowner avoids thereby the burden of debt and the accompanying cost of interest. This also effectively reduces his exposure to the commercial risk since the investor is now carrying part of this. The returns from the venture are however also shared by the investor, whereas under a loan agreement the total income is received by the farmer, from which he then has still to pay interest.

The ways in which investment funds might be used to develop a new scheme are very varied and each will need to be assessed on its own merits and circumstances. In cases such as the provision of a golf driving range or a garden centre it could be that an individual or organisation with an interest in such facilities and also the experience of developing and running them would be looking for suitable farmland sites. A joint company might be formed between the investor and the landowner specifically for the purpose of developing and running the proposed new facility. The amount of capital invested and the duties of each party as regards carrying out the construction and being responsible for its subsequent management would be agreed according to their separate interests and abilities. The share in running costs and in the resulting profits would also be defined by agreement as would the mechanism for dissolving the company or partnership in the future.

Such agreements would need to be carefully prepared, as mentioned in the section on legal issues in chapter 9. It is also of course crucial that the farmer is confident about the reliability of the investors and about being able to work with them. It is possible too for this sort of mechanism to be used between landlord and tenant when converting an old building to an alternative use, although it would be more usual to do this through an amendment to the tenancy agreement as mentioned in section 9.1.2.1.

5.1.4 *Option agreements*

For larger projects, an investor may offer to enter into an option agreement with the intention of ultimately buying the site outright. Although this is essentially an issue of land sales it can arise in the context of diversification schemes and is therefore dealt with further in section 9.1.1.4.

5.1.5 Capital grants

There are currently only few sources of grant aid towards the capital cost of converting part of a farm to a non-agricultural use.

5.1.5.1 Countryside Stewardship and Premium Schemes and Tir Gofal

Under certain circumstances, work that is carried out on a farm may qualify for funding under one these countryside schemes. They tend to be linked to measures that create a public benefit and do not therefore in themselves bring any new income to the farm. The payments are either made as a capital sum on completion of agreed works or annually in respect of ongoing management. The Stewardship Scheme is run by the Countryside Agency in England; the equivalent in Wales of Tir Gofal comes under the Countryside Council for Wales and in Scotland the Premium Scheme is administered by Scottish Natural Heritage.

5.1.5.2 Forestry

Tree planting and the creation of new woods may enhance the environment and even in the longer term improve property values and produce an income, but in the shorter term they show no return. To that extent this would seem a rather altruistic diversification, with little financial justification during the earlier years other than the receipt of grants. For commercial forestry these grants are mostly in the form of capital payments which are made at the time of planting or once established. These are administered by the Forestry Authority under the Woodland Grant Schemes (WGS). When farmland is being given over to trees, these grants would normally come under the Farm Woodland Grant Scheme (FWPS), which is run by the various agricultural departments around the country. These are in the form of annual instalments paid over the first 10 or 15 years according to circumstances. Where better quality land is used, a supplement is payable at the outset which would represent the equivalent of a capital grant. A similar supplement is also available for new plantings in certain targeted areas and for the development of short rotation coppice from poplar or willow. Should the new wood be designed for enjoyment by the local community then it would be likely to qualify also for an initial lump sum payment. The grants that come under the FWPS are all subject to stringent conditions and will not necessarily compensate fully for loss of farming income or changes in valuation but they can be seen as a form of capital contribution towards carrying out the proposed scheme.

5.1.5.3 Objective 5b funding

This source of funding was made available through the European Commission for certain specified areas of Britain but is now due to be replaced. For farm based schemes these are administered by the UK Government agricultural departments, namely the Ministry of Agriculture Fisheries and Food, the Welsh Office and the Scottish Office. Funds are limited and the emphasis of the scheme is primarily to support and develop rural communities rather than to assist individual farm projects, although the latter can be made available under the right circumstances. The qualifying areas are focused in England on the uplands, the south west and on parts of the Welsh border and the eastern coastline, and on many of the more remote areas of Wales and Scotland.

5.1.5.4 Local authorities

In certain cases, grant aid may also be available through local organisations such as the County Councils, Tourist Boards and National Parks Authorities.

5.2 Income

It was seen in chapter 2 that the main incentive for embarking upon diversification tends to be to improve income. There may be occasions when changes are made to a farm without expecting any significant financial return, such as preparing for educational visits by school children through the installation of viewing and safety facilities, but in general it will be future income that provides the key to the whole venture. It may then seem obvious that one should at an early stage work out what these likely returns are to be and an initial analysis will probably have been carried out along the lines described in section 3.1. This now needs to be followed by a more detailed assessment comprising a budget and cash flow such as one would use in any business planning exercise. The fact however that this is for a new and untried enterprise will mean that there are certain special considerations that may have to be taken into account as well.

5.2.1 Budgeted income

Income is a function of the amount of product sold and the price per unit. With a normal farm enterprise it is a relatively straightforward matter to assess such income in that these factors can be quantified by reference to established practice. For example, with an arable crop one knows the area of land being given over to that crop and can estimate the yield per hectare that is likely to be achieved and the probable price at which it will be sold. The various in-put costs that are readily extrapolated from past experience will then be deducted from this.

With a new venture these basic factors may be less easy to define. The amount that is to be sold will depend on how much can be produced, but the figure for this will probably be based on untested estimates. The income will then be determined according to whether that produce can all be sold and at what price. That price may itself be variable, in response to different levels of demand at different times of year. The figures on which such income forecasts are based will be determined by one's interpretation of the market in which the product or service is to be sold. Market research is crucial to setting up any new venture and is dealt with in chapter 7.

Meanwhile, having arrived at a reliable estimate of gross income one still needs to deduct all the costs that are likely to be incurred in realising the product. These are again untested and will be less easy to quantify than in the case of a conventional farming operation. The question of timing can raise another uncertainty; with an arable crop, it is known when harvest will take place and when it would be sold, depending on whether or not it is first to be stored. The input costs too can be anticipated at the particular time when they occur. With a new product, there may be some reasonable assumptions that one can make as to the timing of inputs and of sales, but they may not prove to be quite as reliable as the natural seasons!

It has already been mentioned in chapter 3 that any estimate of income from a new venture will need to assessed against any other existing income that is being foregone. In the example in section 3.2.1 of a suckler herd being given up in favour of a livery stable, the income that would be lost from the cattle can probably be quite clearly identified from the previous farm accounts. There is less uncertainty therefore in this part of the budgeting than in estimating the likely returns from the stables. One must remember to equate like with like and review the past actual figures in the light of the anticipated costs and prices for the year in which the new venture is being introduced.

This example can also be used to illustrate the difference between budgeting for agricultural or commercial returns. Estimating the income from the suckler herd is a matter of knowing the number of calves produced and their likely sale price, together with an allowance for cull cows and replacements and of course all the costs of production. In a commercial venture such as a livery stable there is a further assessment to be made, namely the anticipated occupation rate. It is one thing to have worked out the market rate for renting out each stable but this may then need to be reduced according to the percentage of days in the year when they are actually being used by customers.

The use of budgets in planning a new venture is dealt with further in the context of business appraisal in chapter 6.

5.2.2 Cash flows

Cash flows are a basic management tool for any business, but with a new venture they are perhaps particularly important especially in regard to two fundamental features. When something new is being set up costs are likely to be at their greatest at the outset while income is still developing and those costs and lack of income may well have to be covered by borrowings. A cash flow will demonstrate the extent of this initial imbalance and will make it easier also to arrange properly structured finance.

In farming, the timing of when income and expenditure occurs is relatively predictable; grant payments and milk cheques, for example, are received with reliability on specific dates and payments from grain merchants are also mostly on an acceptable time scale. In other sectors, however, one may have to be prepared for delays in receiving payment from customers, whether commercial, professional or private. This might need to be allowed for when preparing the initial cash flow.

5.2.3 Running costs

A simple calculation of gross income made by multiplying the amount of production by the price at which each unit will be sold provides only part of the answer. From this must then be deducted the operating and fixed costs in order to arrive at the all important bottom line of net income and profit. Such costs can be more difficult to establish than the figures for income as they are not so publicly available. To use the relatively simple examples of livery stables or bed and breakfast, one need only ask people already offering these services to learn what the going rate should be. This might still need to be adjusted to allow for any relevant differences between those examples and one's own proposals, ie features such as location or quality of service. The running costs in terms of wages, feed bills and other expenses are less easily identified and may have to be estimated on a more theoretical basis. Some of these, when still linked to agricultural production, may be found in sources such the *Farm Management Pocketbook* by John Nix, but for most others it will be necessary to research the figures from scratch.

The fixed costs that need to be deducted may well be in the form of an apportionment of those for the whole farm, especially when farm labour and equipment is being used in the new venture. The existing costs are presumably already known and to these may have to be added others that are going to be incurred by the new venture, such as employing additional staff. The apportionment would be made according to an estimate of the amount of time or use of a resource that would be taken up by the venture.

The capital cost of starting up a new business will have been found by one of the means mentioned in section 5.1 above, but it may also be necessary to provide for higher initial operating expenses. The cash flow might be distorted by the fact that production costs will be incurred right from the beginning although the first income may only be received after some delay and without the benefit of any carry forward from a previous trading period. This could result in the current overdraft limit being exceeded for a time so that the existing arrangement with the bank would need to be renegotiated. It is best to have planned for this and to have agreed the necessary provisions with the bank in advance. Not only should this secure the bank's co-operation and advice, but it will avoid the risk of misunderstandings that could trigger an adverse reaction just as the most crucial stage of development.

5.2.4 *Management grants*

Income support from grants is now only very rarely available for farm based schemes. Support payments and other subsidies under the CAP tend still to be linked directly to agricultural production or to land registered for such production. It is intended that the emphasis of such payments should be linked more to environmental and sociological factors rather than to agricultural production and this could become relevant to certain diversification schemes, but at present such funding is still very limited.

5.2.4.1 Countryside Stewardship and Premium Schemes and Tir Gofal

As mentioned in section 5.1.4.1 above, some annual management grants can be available under certain circumstances in respect of costs incurred in the maintenance of special works. The Stewardship Scheme is run by the Countryside Agency in England; the equivalent in Wales of Tir Gofal comes under the Countryside Council for Wales and the Premium Scheme in Scotland is administered by Scottish Natural Heritage.

5.2.4.2 Forestry

As mentioned in section 5.1.4.2 above, new tree planting attracts an annual management grant for 10 or 15 years, depending upon type. This provides some compensation for the fact that the land is unlikely to earn any other income during that time and will instead be incurring some maintenance costs.

5.2.4.3 Non Fossil Fuel Obligation

While this is not a form of direct grant to farmers it does have the effect of subsidising the development of on-farm energy generation, such as windmills. This Government payment is in fact made to the energy generating companies to allow them to pay a premium price for electricity that has been produced means other than oil, gas or coal. This has been instrumental in allowing a number of such alternative sources to be established, but the scheme is guaranteed only for a few years at a time. That limited period must therefore be taken into account when seeking investment finance or borrowings for a project of this kind. One has to ensure that it could still service such financing should the obligation not be renewed at the end of the current term so that the price might then fall to the open market level.

5.3 Check-list

- Obtain or calculate estimates of the total cost of the project.
- Prepare a detailed budget.
- Make enquiries as to the availability and terms of finance.
- Be prepared to make a formal case to potential lenders as to the viability of the new scheme.
- Check that there is adequate collateral to offer as security for the loan and think through what the implications might be.
- If planning to work with an investor, make enquiries as to their status and consider carefully whether one would be happy working with them.
- Check the availability of grant aid.
- If offered an option agreement, take professional advice.

5.3.1 *Sources of advice and information*

- Surveyor/architect
- Building contractor
- Bank/mortgagee
- Financial adviser/AMC Valuer
- MAFF, WOAD, SOAFD, DANI
- Forestry Authority
- Countryside Agency, Countryside Council for Wales or Scottish Natural Heritage
- Trade organisations

Chapter Six

Business Appraisal

Mention has already been made of the importance of preparing budgets and cash flows when planning a new business venture. There can however be particular difficulties about doing this in the rural field where as often as not there may be a double degree of uncertainty. The first is that of not having any previous experience or trading records of the proposed new venture so that one's figures will inevitably rely to a large degree on assumptions and on such evidence as it has been possible to gain through research. Then additionally, the agricultural sector as a whole has been experiencing a period of great change. It is far from clear what costs and prices are likely to prevail and, indeed, what impact there could also be from increased regulations. Budgeting under these conditions is therefore no longer just a matter of taking last year's figures and adding a nominal percentage to costs and making a general assessment of crop and stock prices. It may well be necessary to consider a number of alternative scenarios and to carry out a form of sensitivity analysis.

6.1 Past accounts

Most plans for diversification will begin with a careful analysis of the existing farm business, whether it is being introduced for reasons of improving income or for building on new opportunities. The accounts for the previous two or three years will demonstrate what profit has been made and how this may have varied over that time. These variations will either show an ongoing trend or be explained by particular factors that occurred during that year. Full management accounts will allow one also to identify the performance of each of the individual sectors, separating out for example arable and livestock or each of the different crops being grown on the farm. It should therefore be possible to detect where losses are being made and to consider whether these might be mitigated by improving efficiency or by relinquishing those sectors altogether. To that extent the past accounts will be helpful in showing whether there is a need to introduce a further source of income, as in the cases described in sections 2.1 and 2.2. Farm accounts can, however, have two shortcomings. First, that they are completed often many months after the close of the financial year and may therefore not show a fully up to date picture of the present position. Second, that they are frequently prepared for tax purposes which have a different emphasis to those needed for management.

The distinction between making a profit or loss is of course crucial, but it is not the only issue. Mr Micawber's famous maxim from David Copperfield, whereby income exceeding expenditure by 6 pence produced happiness and expenditure overtaking income by the same amount would bring misery instead, may still be true for a salaried clerk but not for a business using invested capital. The income in that case needs to be more than a source private drawings and must be seen to be showing proper return on capital and a sensible level of gearing or balance between assets and liabilities. Traditionally, the returns on farming and land ownership have been relatively low, particularly when expressed as an investment yield against the value of the underlying property. This was a reflection perhaps of the implied security of land ownership and the limited profitability of agriculture. More recently, as incomes and rents have fallen but while average land prices have remained more stable, the actual returns will have been reduced further. This raises two issues. First, whether it is still acceptable to run one's existing business under such circumstances. Second, that as the diversified venture is likely to be considered less secure and initially unproven, it will need to show higher rates of return on capital than those which have conventionally been accepted on agriculture.

The accounts may well include a balance sheet and schedule of live and deadstock, from which one can gain an indication of the capital that might be raised from the sale of stock or equipment if it were decided to rationalise the business by disposing of one part of it. Such capital could be available for reinvestment in the new venture or otherwise used to reduce some of the existing debt being carried by the farm. Once again, these schedules and valuations may have been prepared for tax purposes and reflect allowances for depreciation which may differ from actual realisable market figures.

The profit and loss account will also show the full cost of bank charges over the year, so that an assessment can be made of the implications of taking out further borrowings in order to fund the new venture. That venture should really be accounted for separately from the farm business but the latter is often relied upon as a means of meeting outgoings such as interest charges during the start up period when the new enterprise is not yet producing any income.

6.2 Budgets

The initial budget provides an indication as to whether the proposed business will be likely to make an adequate profit and show a sufficient return on capital. It will be based on one's best estimates of both income and expenditure and will incorporate crucial assumptions about the price and volume of goods or services sold and the related costs of production. It can be difficult to deduce these figures with much accuracy or confidence, especially in the case of a new and untested business or in a volatile market. To reduce the risks arising from such uncertainties one might be advised to carry out a sensitivity analysis. One approach to this would be to re-run the budget on a "what if" basis, inserting into the calculations for example a lower price per unit or a lesser volume of trade so as to see how the business would perform under those particular conditions. Alternatively, it may be helpful to determine the minimum total return that could be accepted and then to calculate the various price levels or production volumes and costs from which this might be achieved and then see whether these appeared to be realistic market assumptions.

Those assumptions will have been based upon the kind of market research that is outlined in section 7.1 below. While this aims to provide an analysis of prevailing prices, there will inevitably be some uncertainty about being able to gain sufficiently accurate information. Added to this one must also consider the possibility that these current prices might fluctuate during the foreseeable future, if other similar businesses were to start up in competition or if fashions were to change. Some new farming ventures have been victims of their own success while others may have found markets that have expanded beyond their earlier expectations. The development of fish farming, for example, has made commonplace what was previously a luxury food, but this increased supply has resulted also in a major fall in price especially recently when the market was dominated by cheap imports of salmon from Norway. Venison, on the other hand, has not gained the same popularity and deer farming in Britain is still hampered by limited demand and restricted prices.

The costs of production or of providing a service may be a little easier to estimate than the income arising from it, although the question of what volume of trade might be achieved will still be crucial. One might expect such costs to rise in line roughly with inflation, or perhaps also to be reduced through economies of scale as the business grows. One must now be prepared as well for costs to rise due to the introduction of new regulations. Conditions of employment and safety and hygiene measures are being constantly upgraded with the effect often of creating additional expenses that can result in a what was previously a viable business becoming unprofitable.

Timing needs to be considered too. Budgets are like a snapshot of the business over the whole if its financial year. They can of course be revised during that year if it becomes apparent that the original expectations are not being met or that circumstances have changed, but one may also have to make some allowance for the time scale in which targets are being achieved. The initial start up costs will diminish with time but it could be that the income will take longer to generate than originally expected. This may have implications for the financing arrangements, if it were planned to pay off a loan or overdraft within a specified period. One should be aware also that the cost of interest and loan repayments could rise relative to the income from which they were to be serviced, if prices or sales were to fall or if interest rates rose. This raises the issue of whether to opt for fixed or variable rates of interest, as mentioned in section 5.1.2. This matter would normally be decided according to the circumstances prevailing at the time. However in the case of a new venture one may take particular note of the fact that fixed rate loans can be more difficult and costly to change should the development of the business be such as to require unexpected refinancing at some future stage.

Budgeting for a new enterprise will have to assume that it is operating at a certain scale. Yet this is likely to change as the business develops giving rise to different financial positions. When starting small, there may be little opportunity to have an efficient spread of overheads. As the company grows, this situation should improve, until however a stage is reached when the essential expansion requires more investment and a greater commitment, such as employing further staff.

A diversification scheme may well share facilities and their attendant costs with the farm itself, in which case the budget will then have to be prepared for the combined businesses as a whole as well as in a partial format for the new venture on its own. In such situations it may be necessary also to check when each business is likely to come under pressure, either in terms of labour resources or in their cash flow. It would become harder to carry out the cereal harvest on a farm that had introduced a tourist venture which would peak at the same time, ie at the height of the school holidays. On the other hand, there might be a slight financial advantage in that sort of situation as the income from bookings and visitors would probably come in conveniently before the crops were sold so that the overall cash flow would balance out. In other cases one might find that the two businesses faced their heaviest periods of expenditure at the same time, such as when goods or raw materials have to bought in and paid for in the spring when the arable work will also be creating a deficit.

Budgets are an essential management tool through which one can assess the likely performance of a new venture. It will also often form the basis of an application for gaining outside finance. In that context, the figures will give a useful indication of what funding is required and how it will be serviced, but they will not in themselves provide a further piece of information that will be of equal importance to a lender or investor, namely about the management. It is one thing to produce forecasts of profits and returns and another matter to be able to achieve them in practice. If a budget is to give a complete picture of the proposed business it will need to be supported by evidence that the necessary management skills will be available. This may be in the form of a presentation about one's own business experience or abilities or by reference to those of a partner or employee who is being brought into the venture and who has already gained the appropriate expertise from working in that field elsewhere.

6.3 Check-list

- Draw together all the factors involved in setting up the new venture and check again the possible impact on the existing business and the potential for variations. Gain a clear picture of likely returns on capital invested.

6.3.1 *Sources of advice and information*

* Bank account manager
* Management consultants

Chapter Seven

Marketing

Most farmers would associate the term "marketing" with double glazing or insurance rather than some home spun product that is being sold to a small and probably local customer base. It is however one of the most crucial aspects of rural diversification and covers two distinct areas. First, being able to forecast how much of that product can be sold at what price and over what time and, second, the concept of having to sell a product into a competitive market.

In farming, most crops or stock are sold in centralised markets at prevailing prices and there is little that the grower can do to influence the price other than produce the right item to the most appropriate quality at the right time. To present a batch of lambs at market with some advertising slogan or all groomed up as if for a show might be thought of as a form of marketing. However it would cut little ice with the potential buyers who will continue to be influenced only by their own technical judgement and opinion! In most cases too, when a crop is ready to be sold, it will find a buyer and rarely have to be retained on the farm other then if the price at the time were unacceptable to the vendor. Whether it is one variety of wheat or another will not usually make the difference as to whether it is sold or not, even if there may be a marked differential in price. With non-agricultural products, however, there are no such guarantees and no aid payments, and the issues of marketing become inescapable.

Marketing is a huge profession in itself and a subject that can fill volumes of books rather than just a single chapter as in this case. However, other than in the larger and more ambitious projects, the scale of what is normally being planned on a farm will not warrant any extensive market research or promotion and it is therefore the basic principles that need first to be considered in this context.

7.1 Assessing the market

Analysing the potential market for a new product or service is essentially a matter of logic. The fundamental questions to be asked are:

- Is it a product for which there will be a sufficient demand?
- How can that product be presented so that it is best suited to the potential demand?
- Will that demand arise from within an area that is accessible, both in terms of a geographic catchment and on socio-economic grounds?
- What price would people be prepared to pay?
- What would be the cost of bringing the product to that market and what margin would this leave when deducted from the sale price?
- What is the likely level of demand and will there be capacity to meet that demand or, alternatively, is there a risk of over-production?
- Will there be seasonal fluctuations and what effect might this have on maintaining the facilities and employing staff?

Most of us have neither the courage nor the imagination to embark upon a completely new idea and so will probably be looking into something that is already being done elsewhere. In that case, there would then be a number of examples of that type of venture already in operation and one might expect that this would make it easier to assess the market. If someone in the next parish or county is seemingly doing well with a similar business to that which is being proposed, then this would tempt one to assume that it is bound to work on one's own farm too. The same is true also of cases that may have been publicised in the farming journals. There are however so many factors to consider even when the evidence seems to be so clear.

7.1.1 Market evidence

First, the fact that an enterprise is seen to be in full operation does not necessarily mean that it is profitable. It is always possible that an apparently thriving business is in fact being subsidised from another source such as the farm and that without this it would otherwise be making a loss. It may be unusual, and inadvisable, for such a situation to continue beyond the initial start-up period, but it can easily arise if the owner is anxious to justify the original investment and commitment that was made. It could be also that he has a particular affinity with the new business which allows him to treat it almost as a hobby. Although one should be aware of such hidden factors, in the majority of cases an enterprise that has every appearance of running well would be legitimate evidence to encourage one to do the same.

This does not mean of course that can overlook the basic features on which such success would depend. To take a simple example, a farm shop may be thriving because it is in an attractive building in an easily accessible location with convenient parking. It would be much harder to achieve the same number of customers if that shop were tucked away down some side lanes, in an unprepossessing portal framed building on the side of a cramped and muddy yard. There may be more commercial distinctions too; the existing shop, because of its good location, may have been permitted to sell a wide range of goods that has been bought in from off the farm. In the more difficult site, such permission might be withheld and the business would have to survive on home produced goods only. This would have significant consequences, with a lower turnover and a more limited range of customers and greater seasonal fluctuations. If one takes as evidence existing examples of non-farming ventures already operating within the chosen field of business, one must be sure to have identified the differing circumstances between the two and the implications that these might have.

Press articles about diversification schemes can also be very beguiling. Many of them include useful information, although they can be a little one sided in that they tend to deal only with the success stories. It is easy to understand that someone whose new business has failed will be less willing to broadcast it to the media than someone who is proud to show off his achievements! The impression given by press coverage needs to be analysed just as carefully as the kind of market evidence in the case of the better positioned farm shop described above.

Within the farming papers are also advertisements, some of which may be offering new and enticing proposals for diversification schemes. These are certainly a direct source of ideas and of information on such matters. Although one must try to see beyond the immediate impression of guaranteed success and analyse the potential drawbacks as well.

7.1.2 Potential demand

For a product to be successful, it must appeal to a sufficient number of purchasers, be made easily available to them and priced at a figure at which they would be encouraged to buy. This applies equally whether one is offering a service such as bed and breakfast accommodation or selling goods such as Christmas trees or free range eggs. Some businesses are not particularly dependent on location, as in the case of a mail order enterprise or a professional service of some kind. In those instances it will be a matter of defining the range of people who are likely to be interested and the manner in which they are to be targeted.

In most other examples, however, potential demand will be determined firstly by the numbers of people who may be likely to visit the property on which the business is situated and to be interested in buying the product. A farm that is in a picturesque location frequented by visitors from a nearby urban area will therefore have a greater number of potential customers than one that is more remote from a town and lies in a bleak and unpopular area. Numbers alone will not, however, ensure success. The commodity being offered must be of appropriate to them. One can imagine a jewellery designer being attracted to the beauty of the Peak District and setting up a studio in a converted barn that he rents on a farm there. The area is visited by many thousands of people from nearby towns like Sheffield or Manchester and this could encourage him to open a shop from which to sell his latest creations. However, of all those thousands of visitors who are out to see the local countryside, whether by car or on foot, very few would be inclined to buy expensive trendy jewellery. The numbers of people might be there but this would not guarantee a high level of demand for that particular product as it is being offered to the wrong type of clientele in the wrong setting.

On the other hand, if the same barn were used as a shop for wool or sheepskin items or for home cooked cakes and pies, then one might expect a more responsive level of demand. Whether this would in itself ensure economic success is another matter. Although there may be thousands of sheep roaming the local landscape, the product of their skins and fleeces will have been bought in from manufacturers from elsewhere and therefore at a full commercial cost. It may be rather charming to buy something at a farm while on a day's outing or holiday, but the customers will none the less be disinclined to pay more for it than they would for a similar article in town. In this context therefore, the farm shop is competing with the conventional stores who could even be buying similar goods from the same source. The big stores would have the advantage of negotiating better prices with the wholesalers than a smaller retailer such as a farmer, but the latter would at least have the benefit of rather lower overheads than those of staffing a unit in a location such the Arndale Centre in Manchester!

So far, the concept of demand has been considered in terms of one single product or range of products, but there is a further aspect to this that has been described just previously in terms of it being rather charming to buy something from a farm. This refers to the fact that visitors when on holiday or an outing do like to buy something to mark the occasion, either as a momento or to enjoy at the time. This may not be designer jewellery or even sheepskin gloves, but it could be something smaller and relatively incidental such as little ornaments made from local wood or stone or even sweets and ice cream. When working out the market feasibility of a plan to develop a shop for something like specialist woollen goods, the most essential thing will be to estimate the level of demand for these particular items at a certain price level. In addition to that, however, one may be able to reckon on selling a whole range of secondary items as well, such as "local" fudge or postcards and ornaments. As these would all be covered by the same fixed overheads, they would represent not only an extra income but one that came from a slightly different source than the main stream customers and therefore provided a degree of further diversity and effectively of insurance too. Before assuming such add-on activities, it will be necessary to check that they would be acceptable under the planning and other by-law regulations referred to in chapter 8.

It may be more unusual and more difficult to pioneer a completely new idea, as mentioned at the beginning of this section, but the assessment of the potential market will be just as important even though there would appear to be no actual evidence on which to base one's comparisons. In such cases, one would need to determine the possible extent of demand for what is being devised and the price that people would be prepared to pay. This might be done by means of making informal enquiries among a sample of potential customers and gauging their reaction. It could also, when a major enterprise is being planned, involve a more commercial type of market survey. Even where there are no direct competitors in existence, one's research should include a scenario in which someone else were yet to start a similar business in the same area and threaten to take away part of the available demand. This incorporates many of the same principles as before; namely whether the original enterprise is well enough positioned to outperform local competition or whether another similar operation could be developed nearby at some stage in the future but with greater advantages such as being on a better site.

Demand for a product is not always very regular and one may therefore have to work out at what times it is likely to materialise. There could be seasonal fluctuations; after all, few Christmas trees are sold other than in December, and tourists are far more abundant in the summer than in the winter. One needs then to assess not only the level of demand but the time period over which it will be received. This should be matched as far as possible by the dates on which the various in-puts might have to be acquired or paid for and also when staff would be available. Furthermore, an estimate has to be made as to how much of what is being produced would in fact be sold. A clear example of this is found in the relatively straightforward case of bed and breakfast accommodation. Having established the price at which each room could be let, it might be tempting to multiply that nightly rate by 365 so as to arrive at an income figure for the whole year. Would it be realistic however to assume that the guest rooms were going to be used on every night of the year? Even the grandest of hotels have to reckon on only a certain percentage of their rooms being occupied over a year. Some estimate must therefore presumably be made for the occasions when no bookings will have been made. How often this may be over the year is difficult to judge without any first hand experience. The best that one can do is probably to consider the periods of the year when visitors to the area are at their most numerous and the times when they are less evident.

7.1.3 Changing circumstances

In estimating the market potential for a particular product or service, one looks inevitably at the latest evidence of prices and demand. This then forms the basis of the income forecasts for the proposed new business, adjusted possibly with an appropriate inflationary allowance for the coming year. The presumption seems to be that the prevailing conditions will continue for the foreseeable future and that if the budgets work on these latest figures one will be justified in starting up the new venture. It is usually difficult to envisage any major change in circumstances that could upset the financial balance, although there will be occasions when it would be advisable to re-run the budgets on different figures for costs and prices, on "what if"scenarios or as sensitivity analyses. There have in the past been times when crucial market changes have occurred and created unexpected difficulties for those who had recently branched out into diversifications. There can be situations where specific future changes can be identified and used to advantage, as they need not always be negative, but more generally it will be a case of being prepared for the fact that economic circumstances might alter.

With hindsight one can now see how many farm diversification schemes were thwarted by a changing market. In the early 1970s, following a time when foreign travel was made difficult by foreign exchange restrictions, there had been an increase in holidays being taken in Britain and farmers in the traditional areas turned to tourist related enterprises. Soon afterwards, however, an international oil crisis raised the price of petrol and, with the country in recession, fewer people travelled to those former holiday destinations. When the national economic situation improved, cheap package holidays became available so that people were more inclined to go abroad and the British holiday areas took a long time to recover. In the meantime, of course, farms that had diversified into providing facilities were receiving little return on their investment.

In 1989 The Royal & Ancient Golf Club of St Andrews published a report *The Demand for Golf* that came to the conclusion that growing interest in the sport indicated that many more golf courses were required in Britain. Following this there was widespread interest in developing new courses, mostly on what was previously farmland. Meanwhile economic conditions changed and as a consequence demand for membership was reduced in many areas. The newly formed clubs were then unable either to attract the necessary number of new members nor to charge the level of fees on which the development had been originally budgeted. The reduced demand also meant that potential members could become more selective and that courses that were less well located or had inferior facilities faced a further shortfall that might not have arisen had the economy remained strong and fewer courses been constructed.

Changes in markets or in a local infrastructure need not always herald a future downturn but can also allow one to anticipate some new potential. Road improvements, such as to the North Devon Link Road or to the A9 in the highlands of Scotland, can make those local areas easier to reach and thereby more attractive to both visitors and businesses. Along the route, however, farmsteads and villages that are by-passed could suffer a reduction in the tourist and other trade that they had enjoyed before the road was improved.

On a more individual basis, customers' interests can change even if the overall market remains relatively stable. Although people are so often quite traditional and like to return to a familiar situation or to buy a product that they have enjoyed before, there is also a tendency to require something new during their repeat visits. What may therefore have been defined correctly as a marketable commodity at the outset of a venture may need to be adapted in later years if it is to retain the original level of demand.

7.1.4 Competition

Another factor that can change between the initial planning of a scheme and its implementation is the level of competition. A farmer may have identified a particular opportunity and realised that it was not being provided elsewhere within the vicinity. For example, where gravel had been extracted for developing the expansion of a nearby town the resulting pits may have been left flooded with water. One of these being located on the farm might then be stocked as a fishing lake on the assumption that the increased urban population would be looking for such a facility. Although the site is not readily accessible nor particularly large nor attractively landscaped, the farmer decides to proceed with its development by creating the necessary access and parking, introducing the appropriate stock of fish and advertising it in the local papers. As the scheme is modest in size, the investment in creating it is not enormous, but the income from the sale of a reasonable number of licences and tickets would make it viable. However, other gravel pits may also have been excavated in the area, particularly as there was strong local demand for aggregates, and as a result another farmer lights upon a similar idea on an abandoned site on his land. This second property is however more easily accessed and covers a larger surface and has better landscaping. As a result, many fishermen who may have gone to the first site when there was no alternative choice might now abandon it for the newer lake which is easier to get to and offers better sport in more attractive surroundings. The original research into market potential may well have indicated that there would be demand for fishing in the area, but it should also have considered whether it would be vulnerable to another site being developed for the same purpose.

The fact that other similar facilities to the one being planned are already in existence within the same locality, or likely to be developed there, need not always result in untenable competition. By their very nature, many rural businesses lie off the beaten track and visitors or customers will have to turn off a main route and make a detour in order to reach that destination. If that detour were to lead to two points of interest rather than one, the journey may seem more worthwhile. It could therefore be seen as an advantage if a nearby farm were offering some facility that would be attracting a similar clientele to that being sought for the new venture, assuming of course that it was of a complementary nature rather than directly competitive.

Even when there is such competition, a new market opportunity might still be found. For example, a farmer may be keen to convert his land into a golf course, instigated perhaps by his own enthusiasm for the game. He knows however that there are already other golf courses within the area and that it would be difficult therefore to attract a sufficient membership for a new club. But there could none the less be a demand for a pay as you play course from a whole range of people who would not seek to join a club and did not therefore have access to a course.

7.1.5 Defining the product

So far, the financial planning of some form of diversification has been a matter of identifying an opportunity, estimating potential demand and assessing whether the income from it would show an adequate return on the estimated cost of development. At some stage, however, it will also be necessary to check that what is being offered will properly meet the expectations of the targeted customers rather than being designed around the farmer's perception of their requirements. A farmhouse may have been a comfortable family home which now has space to spare that is to be offered as bed and breakfast accommodation. To do so some alterations may have to be made, so as to meet fire and hygiene regulations for example, and it might be assumed that once these are in place no further costs need be incurred. However, in order to attract guests at the right price range and in competition with other places where they might stay, it may be necessary to provide facilities that are comparable with such alternatives. These may be relatively incidental, but none the less important, such as having a television in each room. They could also be of a more major nature such as providing en-suite bathrooms.

In a marketing context, the general principle is to ensure that the product that is being offered will fulfil the customers' expectations rather than reflect just what the producer assumes would be appropriate. The implication is that one should be careful to make enough allowance for the accommodation to be developed to a sufficiently high standard, but it could result in savings too. A house-proud hostess might assume that everything should be to the highest standard, whereas in fact some economies would be perfectly acceptable to the guests. One can envisage a number of features in the bed and breakfast example, whether it be the provision of a bidet in the bathroom or using individual catering packs in the dining room.

7.1.6 Setting the price

For a new product to be successful it needs to be marketed at the right price. Where that product is already being sold by competitors, the price at which it is being traded by them would give a good indication as to what one can charge. If the competition is intense, then it may be necessary to undercut those prices in order at least to get a start. In general the prevailing price will be a useful measure by which to estimate the potential income. There are however occasions when such prices need to be adjusted before being applied to one's own situation. Differences will arise due to location or quality or even the type of clientele to which it is being offered. It is no surprise that a golf driving range in a commuter belt in southern England will be able to have a higher charge per session than one that is near a holiday area by the east coast. Overnight accommodation may always comprise just a bedroom with facilities and a fine farmhouse breakfast. In some situations it will attract visitors who will enjoy a picturesque setting and comfortable furnishings and will pay accordingly. Whereas in other circumstances the guests would be wanting something more straightforward and therefore more economical. These types of distinctions will have to be assessed when gathering evidence of market prices.

The question of price is crucial. Basically, if it is set too high the product will fail to sell and if it is too low it may not cover its costs or make a sufficient profit. There are of course many variations to this over simplified rule and a lower price might be fixed so as to increase the number of sales and create a new level of economies. A lower price might also be justified at certain times in order to keep production or cover overheads going during a slack period. Conversely, prices can be raised at times of higher demand or when there are special opportunities; holiday accommodation is after all always more expensive at the height of the summer season than in February!

The issue of how prices and costs are assessed is dealt with further in section 5.2 on finance and section 6.2 on business appraisal.

7.1.7 Market research

Most farm diversification schemes are on a relatively modest scale, or certainly tend to begin as such. It is to be expected then that such schemes would be instigated on the basis of individual assessments of the market potential following the principles outlined in the preceding sections. It is unlikely that a more formal type of market research would be warranted, due largely to the cost that would be involved and to the fact that rural diversification is often aimed at a local market and against identifiable competition. There are occasions however when such research will have been commissioned by a trade group or some other interested parties and the results then made available to individuals against the payment of a fee that would be more easily justified than the cost of having one's own report prepared. It is not unusual either for local organisations to be formed, such as Farm Attractions Groups, through which such matters of common interest like market potential may be researched. Businesses may be competitive, but they can also be complementary and benefit from collaboration.

7.2 Marketing the product

It was mentioned at the beginning of this chapter that agricultural crops tend still to be sold largely into centralised markets and that farmers have little if any experience of having to promote their own product. When dealing with non-agricultural goods and services or

with specialised crops or livestock, such ready means of sale are
rarely available and it becomes more necessary therefore to use
one's own initiative. This might be quite simple, such as erecting a
sign board at the farm gate, but it can also involve much more
complex issues ranging from advertising and packaging to
contracts and publicity. In many cases professional advice may be
needed; even in the simple example of a sign board just mentioned.
One may not erect just a home-made notice without first checking
the local planning regulations. The actual measures to be taken will
depend on individual circumstances and cannot be listed in any
detail in this context, but an assessment of the general principles
involved should help define the kind of action that is likely to be
required.

Essentially, marketing is a matter of making the product known
to those people who may be interested in buying it. One needs
therefore to identify who these are likely to be and how one might
best attract their attention. Is the scheme of local interest, as in the
case of livery stables where for practical reasons the horse owners
are likely to come from within the immediate vicinity, or does it
have a wider appeal, such as a product that can be sold by mail
order? In the former case, much might be achieved simply by
getting it mentioned in the right local circles, such as among the
hunt and pony clubs, as well as through the vets and blacksmiths.
If advertising is to be used this might need be only through the
local newspapers which would be cheaper and more focused than
some national medium such as *Horse and Hound*. It is also easier to
have the project reported on in the news columns of a local paper
than it would be in a more widely circulated magazine.
Furthermore, if these stables are in a reasonably prominent position
beside a well used road, a sign board would also attract the
attention of potential customers. For a product that depends on
more than local demand, such as for example selling dried meats or
herbs by mail order, these means of marketing would need to be
extended in order to draw in a adequate level of response. For this
it might be more appropriate to circulate promotional leaflets and
order forms on a national mailing list and to place advertisements
in suitable "lifestyle" magazines and other papers.

Identifying the right potential areas of interest will ensure not
only that such marketing is as effective as possible but that it is also
economic. Advertising and other promotional measures are likely
to be costly, particularly if they need to extend beyond the local

neighbourhood, and there is generally no way of knowing beforehand whether they will bring an adequate return. It is therefore important to use them efficiently and to have worked out as best one can the level at which they should be implemented. With too little promotion, there is a risk that it will attract insufficient attention and produce an inadequate response; but if one were tempted to avoid this by arranging a much more extensive campaign it is possible that the response would still fall short of the higher expectations that had been raised and that the greater cost involved would be wasted. Even if a high level of promotion were afforded and did produce a proportionally greater demand, it could be that this would then exceed the planned capacity of supply so that orders would have to be delayed or even cancelled. This would not only be frustrating for all concerned, but could have a seriously negative impact on the way in which the product is perceived in the market place. The right answer will depend very much on the circumstances of each individual case, but a general rule that often applies is to do a little and often rather than rely on one larger single effort.

The success of a new venture rests ultimately upon whether it is something for which there is a demand and whether that demand can be met at a price that will show a worthwhile return. Marketing can play a varying role in achieving this. If the product is one which is readily taken up by the relevant customers, then less promotion would be needed than in the case of something that appears initially to be less sought after by the buying public. The more difficult it is to sell, the more important it will be to have it actively promoted. Such marketing will probably be essential for products or services that are new or for some reason harder to sell. Even in situations where the goods are in sufficient demand and appear "to sell themselves" it could well bring about an improved return. It cannot however be assumed to offer a means of achieving a viable level of sales under any circumstances; if a product has been badly devised or wrongly priced, it is unlikely ever to attract the necessary demand. In those cases, spending money on marketing might only compound a position that was always going to be untenable. One need only think of the old adage about selling refrigerators to the Eskimos!

It should then be decided whether a particular proposal will need to be marketed, and if so by what means and if outside advice is to be taken and from whom. One way of establishing this would be to look at how other similar ventures are promoted and to assume that an equivalent approach would be needed if a comparable or competitive one is to succeed. The manner of presentation will help determine whether this could be done adequately by oneself or whether it would better to use a specialist in order to achieve a suitably professional standard. Such advice, whether in matters of design or of advertising and publicity, tends to involve relatively substantial fees at a time when the business is still only incurring costs and not yet earning any income. One can be tempted therefore to avoid such costs by trying to arrange these marketing matters oneself, but it tends to be an area in which few farmers have any experience and one where it is important not to appear too amateurish, especially in the face of more professional competition. It is an unfamiliar area too in that one would not necessarily know whom to turn to for advice. A choice of agencies will be listed in local directories, but for a more specific recommendation as to whom to use one might be able to ask an existing professional adviser, such as the land agent, whose firm would already be using such services. In some cases these other parties will already have responsibility for marketing, particularly in the letting of residential or business space that may have been created from barn conversions or where franchise or partnership arrangements are used as discussed in chapter 9.

7.3 Check-list

- Estimate the potential demand for the product, by investigating the existing markets in which it is already offered.
- Assess the present competition and the possibility of other producers entering the market in the foreseeable future.
- Establish the optimum price level at which it should be offered in terms of net return as well as total turnover.
- Work out how best the product should be presented and at what level of the market it is to be offered.
- Consider likely seasonal fluctuations and the possible implications on labour resources and cash flow.
- Anticipate changing trends.
- Gather together as much information as possible on the market in which the new product will be operating.
- Assess from examples of similar products the most appropriate means of promotion and advertising.

7.3.1 Sources of information and advice

- Marketing consultant
- Land agent
- Local tourist board
- Local Chamber of Commerce
- Rural Development Agency

Chapter Eight

Planning Regulations

8.1 Planning permission

The issue of planning consent is a crucial one for farm diversification schemes. Not only is it in almost all cases essential to gain such consent but the planning process takes time and needs to be prepared for well in advance. Indeed, it may be advisable to be aware of these matters even some years ahead of the intended development and the reason for this lies in the consultative nature of the present day planning system.

8.1.1 Development plans

As has already been outlined in section 3.4, the overall planning guidelines within each locality are set out in the Structure Plan for the county as a whole and in the Local Plan for the district council areas. These are revised on a periodic basis by public consultation, during which time there would be opportunities for landowners to influence planning policy. This could be either to make a case for some of their own land to be included within areas being zoned for development or alternatively to argue that some other area should not be so designated. To have building development allowed on one's own land offers an obvious financial advantage, but it can in some situations be almost equally important that this be prevented on some neighbouring site. If another site is defined in the local plan as being suitable for development, it would make it far harder to gain planning consent for a similar development on one's own land. But it might also be that the neighbouring development would detract from an existing or proposed scheme such as a conversion of barns into holiday accommodation. A cottage or flat on a farm will attract a larger number of tenants and better rents if it is in an attractive rural setting than if it looked out instead over a new housing estate or light industrial site.

When a site is included within an area zoned for development in the Local Plan it makes it easier to put forward a successful planning application, but the zoning does not in itself guarantee that consent would in fact be granted. It is still possible that other sites in similar situations would be given preference for the time being and that one would have to wait until further pressures in the future for housing or other facilities would encourage the local authorities to allow development on another tranche of land. None the less, participating in the consultation process for the Council's development plans could be a positive way of making it more likely that a proposed diversification would be allowed at some future stage.

8.1.2 Planning applications

Once the relevant development plan is in place, one can establish not only what kind of construction or change of use is likely to be acceptable but also where it would probably need to be located. However, even if a proposal seems to satisfy these general criteria, it can still take many weeks or months for a planning application to be processed. This needs to be allowed for when arranging building contracts or trying to meet special seasonal demands as mentioned in section 3.7. In most cases, the application would best be made by a specialist adviser such as a planning consultant or architect or chartered surveyor since detailed plans need to be submitted together possibly with a well reasoned case. This involves both time and money, and also a degree of publicity. Every application is published in the local press as well as by a notice on the outside of the property and by letter to the immediate neighbours. By making an early application for planning may avoid being thwarted by a delayed start to the development but it does also have the effect of making the scheme public at the same time. This may not matter where there is not going to be any major impact on the local community or where the farmer has already thought to discuss the scheme with those who are likely to be most affected by it, but it could create difficulties where there is a need for confidence or the possibility of local competition.

There is a certain amount that one can establish for oneself before going to the lengths of instructing a professional adviser or making a formal application. Making informal enquiries at the local planning office should provide an indication of the main issues that would be involved, including the question of whether planning permission is in fact going to be required. Planning officers may not be able to give any firm indication as to whether permission would be granted until a proper application is submitted, but they can explain the prevailing policies and highlight potential problems and suggest what the kind of solutions that might be acceptable to the council. Such discussions are generally quite neutral and one would not be in danger of somehow prejudicing the final outcome just by having brought the proposal to the council's attention in this way.

As planning is a relatively logical process, it is possible to anticipate the way in which a new scheme might be treated. A fundamental consideration is whether the proposed development comes within the defined aims of current policy. If one is aware of what that policy is one is able to understand the initial approach that the planning office is likely to take. This will be determined not only by local policy but by national guidelines also, as mentioned in section 8.1.3 below. If the proposal does not conform to those policies, then it will have to be shown to be a legitimate exception to the rule. This can be in a positive manner by demonstrating the advantages that it might bring to the area and in a more defensive way by putting forward solutions to objections that might be raised. It is this latter aspect that often needs to be addressed right from the start. For example, if a scheme is going to involve added traffic in and out of a property that fronts on to a busy road, one may anticipate that the authorities would disallow the development due to the danger or congestion that would be caused by it. One should then be prepared to suggest that an alternative access would to be constructed on to a side road. A new building in a picturesque setting could be ruled out as intrusive if it were proposed on a highly visible site. Yet it might be acceptable if it were to be erected in a more sheltered position and was to be screened by planting some trees. Furthermore, although the cheapest and most practical option might be to construct such a building as a portal frame with steel sheeting and concrete block walling, the planning objections might be overcome by a suggestion that it be clad in local stone and slate or tiles.

The planning authority will also take account not only of prevailing policy but of the opinion of the local community too. People in the immediate neighbourhood of a proposed development, and who are likely to be affected by it, are given the opportunity of making their views known to the planning officer. It would therefore be worth discussing the scheme with those neighbours first, not only as a matter of common courtesy, but so as to have the chance of redesigning it into a format that would resolve some of the possible objections. Local opinions can be forceful and often negative, following the principle now known as NIMBY, or Not In My Back Yard. The planning authority has to put these local views into balance against the needs of the community as a whole and not be unduly swayed by them. However, anything that can be done to make the process less difficult for the planners such as by overcoming potential objections oneself before they are raised, will improve the chances it being successful.

The strength of feeling about development in the countryside can sometimes be such as to lead to powerful arguments being prepared in order to thwart the proposal. There is an increasing body of people who live in the country but who do not make their living from it. They value it for its peace and charm and are concerned about anything that might disturb that environment and are therefore ready to defend it. In doing so they may introduce a wider and more sophisticated range of considerations than would normally be expected in the case of a farm scale development, such as using the support of rural pressure groups or the services of special consultants and even of barristers. Such measures may not necessarily sway the planning process but the applicant will need to be ready to go to the lengths of presenting a comparable case in order to counter them.

Planning applications are made to the planning officer for the relevant local council. The matter may then be decided upon either by such officers themselves or referred to the planning committee according to the circumstances. That committee is made up of elected councillors and it could be useful for an applicant to have found out who those councillors are and as to whether there are any particular local connections or interests. In some of the larger or more contentious cases, these committee members can find themselves being lobbied by interested parties, especially by those who are objecting to it. There can be occasions too when the scale and importance of the proposed development is such that the planning committee will refer the matter to a meeting of the full council. Planning is administered by the district or county council, but reference is also made to the parish council, whose members will be more local to the site being developed and who will also be more likely to be known to the applicant. In most cases of farm diversification, the planning decision will be made on clearly technical and procedural grounds and there will be no purpose in trying to bring any extra influence to bear. None the less, it is as well to be aware of how the process is conducted and how other parties may respond.

If an application is refused, one has a right to appeal to the DETR (Department of the Environment Transport and the Regions). This would introduce a further sphere of activity that relies even more heavily upon procedure and would need the involvement of professional advisers not only just in planning matters but sometimes also in matters of law too. On a slightly less draconian level, however, when an application is refused it may be on specified grounds and there could then be opportunity to resubmit another application that addresses those items and is therefore likely to be accepted.

In some cases, particularly where a larger development is proposed, it is possible that consent will be granted only on condition that the applicant fulfils certain special requirements. These may range from planting a screen of trees to contributing towards the construction of a new road junction. If this were to arise, then an allowance needs to be made for the additional cost and time that would be incurred.

8.1.3 Government policies

Although planning matters are administered by the local councils, they come within guidelines set out by the national Government and now also the Scottish Parliament and the Welsh Assembly.

Within England and Wales, these issues are set out in a set of Planning Policy Guidance Notes known as PPG7. This recognises the reducing role of agriculture in the country and encourages diversification as an alternative, especially where it brings economic benefits in the form of creating employment or attracting visitors. Individual applications for such developments can therefore be presented in the context of subscribing to the principles of PPG7 even if they do not come within the more particular designations of the local Plans. In Scotland, similar principles apply and are even supported with grant aid that can be made available for the conversion of agricultural buildings to alternative use and for rural housing developments.

8.1.4 Land classification

Another Government measure affecting rural planning is that of Land Classification as defined in the maps produced by the Ministry of Agriculture Fisheries and Food for England and Wales and by the Macaulay Institute in Scotland. These tend now to be used as a measure of land quality in such contexts as agents' sale particulars, but their original purpose was to provide guidance for planning authorities. Although circumstances have changed since the introduction of these maps in 1976 and agricultural production no longer has the same degree of priority, planning authorities have still been required to take account of land quality. This whole principle is now due to be reviewed, but at the present time councils continue to be discouraged from allowing development on the better types of farmland if other sites on more ordinary land may be used instead. A planning application involving a site that is classified as Grade 1 or 2 (or Class 1 or 2 in Scotland) will therefore be more difficult to agree than a comparable scheme on land of a lesser quality. It may not be possible for an individual landowner to select a site according to its classification and indeed the area of land in Britain that is classified as Grade 1 and 2 is relatively limited, so that this issue will only arise in a minority of cases. None the less, it is an aspect of planning policy that can be usefully assessed in advance. Either in knowing that a special case will have to be made because the site is Grade 1 or 2, or alternatively in being able to promote it as a good opportunity to use Grade 3 land in a locality where the preponderance of land is of a higher quality.

8.1.5 Scheduled monuments

One can often see throughout the country small areas of rough grassland that appear to be farmed in only a limited fashion. One might then think that these could be well suited for an alternative use, being of little value to the farm and certainly not of a high classification. In fact, the reason why many of these sites are uncultivated is that they overlie some ancient monument which cannot be disturbed by ploughing. It follows then that the authorities could not permit any construction work in such an area and that an application for development would hardly be likely to succeed. Most of these monuments are protected in this way merely to prevent any damage to archaeological evidence rather than that they have much interest or appeal to the general public.

In some cases, however, they might have a wider attraction so that there could be scope for developing a visitor centre nearby. In such circumstances, the planning authorities could well be able to take a positive stance towards a proposed development on the basis that it would be providing tourists with suitable facilities. This would of course be on the understanding that the building works took place on an adjacent site to the monument itself and were done to an appropriate design and finish.

8.1.6 Trees

There are two main ways in which trees can be governed by planning regulations. First, as to whether they can be removed and, second, as to whether new ones need to be planted.

Where a group of trees is to be felled in order to create a site for a diversified enterprise, an application would have to be made to the Forestry Authority for a felling licence. Where such felling takes place as part of the normal woodland management, the licence will be granted only on condition that the area is replanted with trees under an approved plan. If the site is intended for a development that has the support of the planning authority, it may be possible for this requirement to be adapted so that the new trees would be planted on an alternative site or on a lesser area. Even where only a few individual trees are to be removed, a licence will be required if the amount of timber taken exceeds 5 m^3 in any one quarter, which is the equivalent of about two large trees or five half grown or semi-mature ones. Even if it is only a single tree that is to be removed or a small number that amount to less than the size specified for licence, one may be prevented from felling if they have been made subject to a Tree Preservation Order (TPO).

This may occur where a tree or group of trees has a particular historic or scenic value, or even where an application was made for a TPO and approved by the local authority. Such an application might be successfully made by a member of the public who has reason to suspect that the trees might be removed and has been able to make a sufficiently strong case for preservation to the local council. Trees that have been so protected cannot then be felled without the consent of the local authority. It could arise therefore that when it becomes known that a new development is being planned and that it will involve the removal of a few trees, someone could apply to the council to have those trees made subject to a preservation order. The existence of such an order need not rule out all hope of gaining planning consent for the proposed development but it would make it more difficult for the council to grant such consent.

One cannot prevent people taking a protective view of trees and of wishing to preserve them, often regardless of whether or not they are worthwhile specimens. One can be prepared for such public reactions and chose an alternative site or suggest some acceptable compromise such as planting new trees elsewhere.

Indeed, new planting can be imposed as a condition of being granted planning permission but can also be undertaken by the landowner's own initiative. If consent is being sought for a new building in a site that is rather visible to the public, it may well be that the planning authority will ask for a group of trees to be planted as a screen to hide the development. Such screens can also be planted voluntarily by owners themselves, to grow between a site on which potential development is anticipated. This would be mainly to hide the future building work from their own view but also to create what will by then appear to be a natural boundary. If the proposed development site is already effectively separated from the farmland by a belt of trees, the planning authority should find it easier to grant consent.

Therefore, in preparing to apply for permission for a particular development, one should anticipate the various constraints that might arise in relation to standing trees or to planting new ones. On a longer term basis one could also find opportunities to plant trees now as a strategic barrier around a future development site.

8.1.7 Traffic

Development on a farm will often result in an increase in traffic going to and from the property, whether due to visitors or employees or from deliveries and despatches. As often as not this traffic will have to pass along relatively narrow country lanes and perhaps also through the nearby village. A planning application is therefore not only a matter of determining whether the proposed building works can be permitted but whether the local road system is will be able to absorb the extra traffic. There are two particular problems associated with this.

First, whereas it is often possible to modify a building design in order to make it more acceptable to the planning authority, if the roads are too narrow one has little scope for suggesting a remedy. With major developments, such as a new supermarket on a greenfield site, this can sometimes be resolved by the developer undertaking to fund all or part of such road improvements as might be necessary to alleviate the problem. Larger commercial developments are now sometimes linked to the provision of bus services or car sharing schemes. These would however usually be well beyond the financial scale of an on-farm diversification scheme and one's plans must therefore be workable within the constraints of the existing road system. Second, local opinion will tend to be strongly against any proposal that would involve an increase in traffic along the country lanes, since far more people would feel affected by that than by the development itself. The planning authority takes note of such public opinion, as already mentioned in section 8.1.2 above, and will tend to be understandably influenced by the numbers who had expressed their views on the matter. Furthermore, there is now widespread concern among national and local government agencies about the proliferation of cars in the countryside and the lack of alternative public transport and this can also affect the position of the planning authority.

In most rural diversification schemes, the resultant increase in traffic is modest and may be outweighed by the fact that it is seen to be providing a worthwhile contribution to the local economy. It is none the less an issue which would need to be thought through at an early stage.

8.1.8 Noise

With planning matters one tends to think mostly of the proposed building works and the visual impact that they would have on a rural environment. There is however also the potential disturbance from noise, that can be particularly acute in a quiet country setting even if whatever is being carried out within the former farm buildings is not especially loud by industrial standards. Again, this is a sensitive issue to local residents and one that would have to be reckoned with where undue noise is likely to occur. Noise tends also to travel further in the country than in an urban environment and even if, for example, a clay pigeon trap is sited in a remote spot away from any immediate housing, there could still be a sufficient degree of disturbance to influence the planning decision. It is difficult to reduce the amount of noise of some activities such as light industry or motor sports other than by choosing a sufficiently remote location. It is however sometimes possible to compromise by accepting a reduction in the time that the activity may be carried out, such as only within strict working hours for an industrial process or on a limited number of days each year for a sport such as shooting or motorbike scrambling. Restrictions of this kind do of course have financial consequences, either in making a building more difficult to let or in the income that would be received from a leisure pastime that can be used only for a limited time.

8.1.9 Designated areas

There are certain designations that can be applied to an area and within which then special consents are required before any development can be carried out.

8.1.9.1 Conservation Areas

This is applied mostly to towns or villages that still have a high proportion of historic or period houses. Any new development within such an area would need to be in keeping with the age and style of the existing buildings. This could mean that a construction such as a portal framed lean-to would not be permitted, even though it might have been acceptable elsewhere, and that if consent were granted it could be on the condition that the owner uses sympathetic materials such as stone facings to the walls and proper tiles on the roof. When situated within a conservation area, one needs therefore to weigh up the fact that planning consent could be more difficult to achieve and that it might involve special conditions that would make the building work more expensive than would otherwise be the case.

8.1.9.2 Areas of Outstanding Natural Beauty (AONBs)

As the name implies, this refers to specific landscapes that have a special attraction and are relatively unspoilt. In planning terms there are additional restrictions on new development within an AONB, regarding where it may take place and as to what design features it should incorporate in order to limit its impact on the local environment. Therefore, for someone whose property is situated within an AONB it will mean, as in the previous case of conservation areas, that the question of planning permission will need extra consideration as to whether it will be granted and what constraints or additional costs might then be incurred. Policy relating to AONBs is administered by the DETR in England and by the Welsh and Scottish Offices respectively. Local planning matters in these areas are however still determined by the county and district councils subject to the overall guidelines laid down by the Government agencies.

8.1.9.3 National Parks

In effect similar to AONBs, in that these parks cover areas of landscape and amenity value. They are in fact administered by a different authority, The Council for National Parks, but the implications for town and country planning are similar to those for AONBs.

8.1.9.4 Sites of Special Scientific Interest (SSSIs)

Not perhaps so readily recognisable as AONBs, the SSSIs are imposed upon certain areas in which, as the name implies, there is some feature of rarity or of botanical or zoological importance that needs to be protected. Such protection generally means being left undisturbed even by agricultural or forestry practices, let alone a new development. It would seem then unlikely that one could gain planning consent in an area that has been so designated. Although there may be occasions when the designation was made over a whole area such as a wood or parcel of pasture whereas the items to be protected are found only in one small part of it. In that case, it is possible that some changes may be permitted on the less vulnerable areas, although inevitably subject to certain restrictions regarding for example access or noise.

8.1.9.5 Green Belts

These are designated by the local planning authority and are defined on the relevant development plan. They have been created on the edge of certain towns and cities with the purpose of adding an extra constraint upon development. Planning applications on properties lying within a green belt will therefore tend to be resisted, although rural diversification may well be permitted, especially if it provides a service to the adjacent urban population, such as a pick-your-own enterprise or a farm shop or zoo.

8.1.9.6 Environmentally Sensitive Areas (ESAs)

Although sounding in name as if these areas would carry similar constraints and requirements to some of those listed above, they operate at present still on a voluntary basis and do not impinge formally on local planning policy.

8.1.9.7 Other designations

Further restrctions might apply in certain cases under European Commission schemes such as Special Protection Areas (SPAs) and Ramsar sites. These tend however to be in marginal areas that are favoured as breeding or feeding grounds for birds and are unlikely to impinge upon diversification plans other than in a coastal location where tourist activities might have been considered.

8.2 *Building regulations*

Most building work, whether a new construction or an alteration, will have to satisfy certain regulations that are administered by the local authority but which are quite separate to planning permission. The main implications for someone embarking on a diversification scheme are twofold.

First, that one can no longer rely just on one's own judgement as to whether a building can be extended or adapted to another purpose. Traditionally, such work would have been planned and executed using the farmer's own skill and labour. This is certainly still an option, as the regulations are concerned only with how the work is done and not as to by whom, but it can mean that a proposal which appears to be perfectly practical might in fact fail to satisfy the official requirements and therefore be disallowed. These cover a whole raft of issues such as headroom and ventilation and types of materials. It may be, for example, that in providing bed and breakfast accommodation one needed to put a shower room into an empty roof space at the end of a landing. There might seem to be enough space for the various fittings to be installed and then operated, but if the sloping ceiling meant that the headroom was less than that allowed by the regulations, then the whole project would have to be abandoned or repositioned to another part of the house. It is important therefore to check at an early stage that one's plans would comply with the regulations and whether, if they did not so, it might be still feasible to proceed subject to making some adjustments and then at what additional cost.

The second factor of having to comply with regulations is that it introduces a degree of formality to what might previously have been just a personal initiative. Before beginning work it will be necessary to submit to the Council either a set plans of the scheme or an official notice. The former needs to be in full detail, and therefore probably prepared by a surveyor or architect and incurring the attendant costs. The latter can be made with less detailed plans and might therefore seem to be the easier option. However, using the system of just serving notice does rely upon one having a detailed knowledge of the regulations. It should really only be used when the work is being carried out by someone sufficiently experienced in such matters, such as a builder or contractor, rather than the farmer himself.

Whichever system of notification is used, the council will expect to carry out a series of inspections as the work reaches particular stages, such as digging foundations or connecting the drainage. Where detailed plans are made available, any potential faults in the design or specification can be identified in advance and then raised by the building control office of the council so that the builder can make whatever alterations are required. With the alternative procedure of serving notice, any queries made by the council will only become known at the time of inspection when it will probably be difficult and costly to rebuild the work already done. The option to serve notice rather than submit detailed plans is in any case not available if the project is such that it becomes subject to fire regulations, as would be the case when visitors are invited into the converted building.

Farming is already sufficiently bedevilled with form filling and red tape and it could be tempting therefore to ignore further bureaucracy and just carry out the work without giving the council any notification. This would not only lead to the possibility of prosecution and payment of a penalty, but would also involve some legal issues. Normally when work is completed to the inspector's satisfaction, a certificate is issued by the council. At such time as the property were to be sold in the future, purchasers might well expect to see evidence that modern alterations were done to the required standards. If none were forthcoming, the purchasers might not proceed except at a discounted figure or on the understanding that a retrospective certificate is obtained. While this last option is available, it would involve difficulties, costs and delays, none of which would be welcome in the middle of a sale negotiation. In most cases, there would be no intention of selling the property within the foreseeable future, but the lack of a certificate might still come to light. The converted building may be being used for a purpose that relies on a public awareness, whether through advertising or word of mouth. One's custom for bed and breakfast accommodation, for example, will mostly depend on advertising and reputation and such promotion could easily come to the attention of the building control office. Ultimately too there is the liability to members of the public on one's property. Using again the example of bed and breakfast accommodation, if a guest was injured in a fall down stairs and it was discovered that the stairs had been constructed without a Building Regulations Certificate, the owner would be held directly responsible.

In short then, the consequences of not following the proper procedures as regards Building Regulations could be crucial. In following these procedures, one will not only have to prepare plans and technical descriptions but also allow for an element of time delay before being able to start work. If the project is one that depends upon being ready at a certain moment, such as the beginning of the holiday season, the additional timing will need to be planned in advance.

8.2.1 Listed buildings

Buildings that are listed as being of architectural or historical interest are subject to additional controls as regards building alterations. The constraints imposed by this depend upon the grade of listing and on the individual circumstances. This would apply mostly only to period houses and traditional buildings, although some more modern structures can also be listed if they are deemed to be of sufficient significance – even a Nissen hut might now be considered worth preserving as an example of wartime architecture! Certainly where period properties are involved, it would be as well to check their status with the local planning authority in case this were to restrict one's proposal or give rise to additional costs through the need to use traditional materials.

8.3 Environmental Impact Assessments

Where a major development is proposed in a rural setting, it is possible that the local authority will require that an Environmental Impact Assessment is carried out. This is a means of establishing how much the scheme would disturb the existing agricultural and natural landscape and to weigh up also what advantages it might bring. These are rarely required for on-farm diversification although a recent EC Directive has widened their application to include a greater range of intensive livestock businesses.

8.4 Check-list

- Check local development plan.
- Have informal discussion with local planning officer.
- Review the proposals and the site in the light of the above.
- Where appropriate, check the position with the local highway authority.
- Discuss proposal with neighbours and other affected parties.
- Check with architect/surveyor that building regulations can be met.
- Consult adviser and prepare planning application ensuring, where appropriate, that it anticipates likely objections.

8.4.1 *Sources of information and advice*

- Local planning office
- Local highway authority
- Land agent/architect/planning consultant

Chapter Nine

Legal and Tax Aspects

It is unlikely that a new initiative such as a diversification project would be undertaken without reference to a solicitor and probably also an accountant. This section serves only to introduce the kind of topics that one may need to prepare for and cannot give definitive answers to legal or fiscal questions. These issues may be considered in three main categories:

(i)   the tenure of the property itself
(ii)   the occupation or management of the new scheme
(iii) national legislation and local by-laws

9.1 Tenure

This covers the interests of freeholders (feuhold in Scotland), whether as landlords or owner-occupiers, and of tenants. Some of the issues may be of equal relevance to all three categories and others will be specific to the separate positions of landlord or tenant.

9.1.1 Freehold (and Feuhold)

This form of ownership is largely unfettered and as such it could be assumed that one would be able to do whatever one wished within the confines of the property provided that it did not infringe the law of the land. There are however a number of points that may need to be checked even by those who own their properties outright.

9.1.1.1 Shared access and services

It is not uncommon for rural properties to share an approach road or driveway and even to be linked to the same private water supply. There may then be agreements or restrictions on the use of these common facilities, effectively preventing either of the parties from using them for anything other than farming or domestic purposes. This could result in the proposed scheme having to be abandoned, or in having to make provision for building a new and independent access, or at least in having to come to some negotiated settlement with the neighbour. Even where a wider commercial use is permitted, it might be necessary to revise the agreements for maintenance so that they reflect the greater usage by the property on which the diversification has taken place.

9.1.1.2 Restrictive covenants

Even where a property is owned freehold (or feuhold in Scotland), it could be subject to a covenant whereby the occupier is restricted from carrying out certain specified matters without the consent of the other party. This can arise where a farm was once bought off an old estate or where a new farmhouse has been built close to the original one which was then sold on as a separate property. Again, these covenants can effectively prevent any new development taking place or otherwise mean that it could only proceed following a negotiation with, and presumably payment to, the person benefiting from the covenant.

9.1.1.3 Mortgage contracts

A landowner may well have a mortgage on the property that was made on the condition that the property is used only for agriculture. This may have been to satisfy the statutes of the mortgagee as in the case of the Agricultural Mortgage Corporation. It may have been to provide some form of control for the lender who had made the loan on the strength of the borrower's farming expertise. Such conditions are unlikely to be as constraining as those mentioned previously. They would probably not apply to the introduction of a minor diversification being run in conjunction with the original farm business, but they would need to be cleared before any firm commitments were made.

9.1.1.4 Option agreements

As mentioned in section 5.1.3, option agreements will tend only to arise with larger development schemes rather than on the more usual on-farm diversification. However, it could occur where an outside organisation were to be interested in investing in a scheme, either through buying the property once it has the benefit of planning consent or by perhaps entering into a joint venture. Such investors would prefer to postpone having to buy the land until they had secured the necessary planning permission. The process of gaining consent for larger and more controversial developments can be both lengthy and expensive. The applicants will therefore wish to ensure that they would have the exclusive rights to carry out that development once they had secured the necessary consents. This can be done through an agreement that binds the landowner to sell on the property to them under certain specified conditions. In return the landowner is likely to be offered an initial payment or fee, which will be a relatively nominal amount compared to the ultimate value of the site with planning permission but which can still seem attractive to the farmer at the time. These option agreements can take various forms and can incur differing commitments on the two parties involved. They certainly need to be negotiated with care and should involve the professional help of an agent or solicitor.

9.1.2 Tenanted farms

Changes being made to tenanted farms can be instigated by either landlord or tenant but will, in both cases, normally require some form of written agreement.

As it is the tenants who run the farm business and have exclusive occupation of the land and buildings, one might expect that they would always be the ones to introduce the diversification. There are however situations where landlords might take such an initiative as in the example of some unused buildings that could be converted to a non-agricultural purpose. The landlord may have the resources to invest in such a scheme and thereby create a return from a part of the property that was of little value to the farm, but he does not automatically have the right to do so. He would need to draw up a supplementary agreement to remove the buildings from the original lease and perhaps also to revise the rent or pay some compensation, even though the buildings were no longer of much use to the tenant. Matters of access and shared services would have to be formally defined as well. When planning such a scheme, landlords will therefore need to check not only the legal requirements but also the stance likely to be taken by the tenant.

For tenants there are two main considerations; ensuring that they observe the terms of their agreement and protecting the capital that they would be investing in land or premises that are after all attached to the landlords' property.

9.1.2.1 Tenancy agreements

Many traditional tenancy agreements include a clause effectively restricting the use of the property to agricultural purposes, in which case the tenant would be well advised to obtain written consent from the landlord before embarking on a diversification scheme. All agreements made after September 1995, as Farm Business Tenancies, would be likely to have specific provisions on the question of commercial activities being run on the premises. Most agricultural leases will also contain a clause preventing the tenants from subletting any part of the property without landlords' consent. Where a new venture is going to be run by an outside party on some form of rental agreement, it would need to be cleared first with the landlords. Normally, such consent cannot be unreasonably withheld and this should not therefore endanger or delay the project, but the tenants would be in breach of the terms of their lease if they had not made a formal application to the landlords. It would also not usually incur the payment of a premium or other financial consideration to the landlords which could have increased the initial cost of the scheme to the tenants, although it might well be reflected in the level of rent demanded by the landlords, either at the time of granting the consent or at the next review. In those cases where the development was being funded by the tenants alone, such increases would be limited to the degree by which the increased income had been facilitated by the use of the landlords' property. They could only incorporate an element of return on capital if the landlords had participated directly in the scheme either by a joint investment with the tenants or by funding it outright.

9.1.2.2 Compensation

Where tenants are investing their own capital in some development on their landlords' property they will need to ensure that they would be properly compensated for this were they to leave the holding while those capital improvements still had a positive value. It is customary therefore for some form of depreciation to be agreed over the economic life of the development. If, for example, some of the farm buildings were being extended or converted, it might be agreed that the cost of those works should be written down over a specific period such as 20 years. If the tenants were to vacate the holding before then, after perhaps only 10 years had elapsed, then they would be entitled to be paid back a sum equivalent to half of their original investment.

This payment would be the responsibility of the landlords, who must therefore be aware of the implications of accepting such an arrangement. It has in the past been unusual for tenants to give early possession of let farms. Were they to do so, the landlords would gain the full vacant value of the holding and would have three options available to them: to sell the land or to take it in hand, whether directly or under contract, or to relet it.

If a farm that has been developed with some form of diversification were to be sold with vacant possession, it would command a premium over the value that it had when tenanted. That premium price would presumably provide sufficient funds for the landlords then to pay out the compensation that would be due. It is always possible, however, that the diversification would not appeal to such buyers and that the price that they were offering for the farm would not therefore fully reflect the costs that had been incurred in developing the scheme in the first place. This might not be crucial in the case of landlords selling with vacant possession, but it could be of greater consequence if the farm were being relet and the landlords were relying on getting from prospective tenants a premium on entry to pay for the improvements. If, just as with the in-hand buyers, the new tenants were unable or unwilling to justify the full amount of compensation the landlords would have to make up the shortfall. Were the landlords to take the land in hand, they would of course need to fund the compensation in full themselves, just at a time when there would be taking on other financial commitments such as providing working capital. The enterprise that had been introduced by the former tenants might have been rather specialised and therefore difficult to take over or it may not have been well suited to that particular farm. It has already been mentioned that it is unusual for let farms to be vacated and it might well be that this arose because the new venture was unsuccessful and then resulted in the outgoing tenants having to give up their holding. Under the terms of most agreements the landlords may be expected to give their consent to an improvement proposed by the tenants, but they will nonetheless need to consider carefully the question of compensation and of the effect on freehold value.

9.1.2.3 Future expansion

A new venture may well be developed in stages, beginning with a limited initial operation which would be expanded into a fully commercial enterprise at a later stage once it has proved to be successful. The tenants will need to be sure that such expansion will available to them when required in the future and they may therefore be advised to provide for this when seeking their landlords' consent for the original scheme. It would be unfortunate if the essential further development of the project were to be thwarted due to difficulties in gaining additional permission from the landlords.

9.1.2.4 Sublettings

Where subtenancies are being created, these will have to be formulated in such a way that they cannot overrun the term of the original lease. At whatever moment the farm tenants were to vacate the farm, whether at the termination of a fixed term agreement or on retirement or other voluntary arrangement, they would be responsible for giving full possession of the holding. Prior to that, while still in normal occupation of the property, they would also be responsible for ensuring that the sub-tenants do not infringe any of the terms of the main agricultural lease. Sublettings are therefore normally best made using the correct legal forms such as shorthold tenancies and holiday lettings or commercial leases under the Landlord and Tenant Acts.

9.1.3 Licences

In some situations where part of a farm is being used by another party for a non-agricultural purpose such the grazing of horses, a licence may be suggested as a less formal alternative to subletting. This will however again have to be arranged in the proper legal format, taking care particularly that it could not be construed at any time as having created a tenancy. One requirement for this would be that the licence is for a term of no more than two years and, although they can be renewed at the end of each term, the lack of any longer term security could be a problem to someone setting up a new business. The farm tenants will also need to have checked that such a licence did not infringe the terms of their own lease agreement.

9.1.4 Franchises

Franchising can be a useful means for someone to gain a start in a new business, but is more commonly found in the field of retailing or the sale of services than in on-farm diversification. It could however apply to a situation such as the development of a garden centre or specialised farm shop. The franchisee acquires through payment of a fee, the right to sell a product or service that bears a particular brand name and is supported by marketing and other resources. The income thus earned will then normally attract a further fee payment in the form of a royalty or dividend to the company that owns the product. The franchisee has the advantage of being supplied with a well known commodity and of being advised or directed as to how best to sell it. However the legal agreement on which it is based can be complex and would best be assessed by a solicitor.

9.1.5 Partnerships and joint ventures

Where a new enterprise is introduced on to the farm by an outside party, it may well be on the basis of a collaboration between the farmer or landowner and the person running the business. They are likely each to have their defined roles with, for example, the farmer providing the property on which the business is to be run and the other party owning the stock and perhaps having responsibility for the day to day management. The arrangement can then either involve them both fully in the business, as in the case of a partnership, or allow them still their separate functions. In the latter case the landowner is rewarded with the equivalent of a rental return and the manager is entitled to the remaining profit. Under a partnership, they will share all the liabilities together, whereas in a less formal joint venture their responsibilities remain limited to their own area of involvement. In either instance, a formal agreement will be needed to avoid the possibility of problems or misunderstandings in the future.

9.1.6 Arrangements with occupants

Within the legal agreements, there will also need to be provision for a number of practical issues that are likely to arise.

These will included arrangements as to the access that the new occupiers will be entitled to use to reach their part of the property and also how the main services will be provided and accounted for. There may be a need to define certain restrictions as to the hours during which the premises may be used and the level of noise or other disturbance that would be associated with it. This might be not only for the convenience of the occupiers of the main property but also for their immediate neighbours. Furthermore it would protect against any diminution in value that could be caused by the presence of some noisy or unattractive commercial activity. Where such matters are anyway the subject of conditions imposed in the granting of planning consent, these will have to be made to be binding directly upon the occupants themselves.

The legal agreements will also be likely to require the occupants to be fully liable for all matters related to their activities and to be properly insured.

9.1.7 Creation of tenancies

Where a converted part of the farm or estate is let out to a tenant, a formal agreement will have to be prepared in line with the relevant legislation, whether under the Agricultural Tenancies Act, the Landlord and Tenant Acts or the Housing Acts. Each will have their separate implications as to the terms of the agreement, particularly with regard to the possibility of regaining possession in the future. The creation of a tenancy could also impact on the capital value of the property as a whole. Tenanted farmland has always commanded a lower price than that with vacant possession. While this may not be critical where only a minor part of the property has been let to a new and potentially lucrative use, it should be checked before entering into any long term lease. The fact that part of a holding is no longer accessible to the farmer because it is let to a third party could be considered a disadvantage to some potential purchasers. This could reduce the price that they would have been prepared to pay, even if it is producing a useful non-agricultural rental income.

9.2 Regulations and requirements

A farm or estate will already be subject to certain regulations governing safety and hygiene, determined largely by the Health and Safety at Work Act and the COSHH Regulations (Control of Substances Hazardous to Health). A non-farming enterprise will face similar requirements, according to the nature of the business. This is especially the case when dealing with food processing or retailing or when the public is being invited on to the property. These will of course have to be complied with from the outset. Advice may need to be sought from the local authority as to what measures will have to be implemented. Such regulations are not just confined to physical factors such as whether dangerous machinery is adequately protected or food is stored in a sufficiently safe manner, as they can also determine the ability of the people running the business. For example, pony trekking, paint balling and similar pastimes may need to be licensed by the Adventure Activities Licensing Authority before the facility can be opened to the public. In addition the person running the venture will have to demonstrate not only that it is properly equipped and well designed, but that they themselves are competent to manage it. If this were to involve undertaking some training so as to be able to demonstrate the necessary skills and experience, then this might have a further benefit in being able to secure a reduction in insurance premium.

9.2.1 Insurance

The property's insurers will probably need to be informed of any change of use, again particularly if it involves the public or the handling of foodstuffs or the introduction of new equipment. In most cases this would result in just a straightforward change in the cover provided and possibly also a corresponding change in premium. Some activities might however require special consideration, especially if those that introduce a greater element of potential risk, such as clay pigeon shooting or paint balling.

9.3 Taxation

Taxation is unlikely to be a prime consideration when planning to diversify a farming business, although there will be some aspects that may need to be taken into account.

Agriculture and agricultural property currently benefit from relatively favourable treatment, especially as regards capital taxation. Some of these advantages could be lost if there were to be a significant change in the nature of the business away from farming. Of particular note is the relief allowed against agricultural property for Inheritance Tax purposes. If all or part of the farm is being given over to non-agricultural uses, it would be as well to structure the arrangement so that this tax relief would still apply. This could also arise where because of a reduction in the farm business following diversification, the land is to be farmed by another party.

Business rates would become payable on that part of the property given over to a commercial use and would have to be budgeted for.

It may be advisable to have a separate VAT account for the new venture particularly in the initial stages when there could be a greater number of inputs being acquired for the business.

At present unearned income, such as that received from rents, is taxed no differently to that gained from one's own in-hand business. This did at one time attract a higher rate of tax and those farmers arranging lettings on their diversified properties might want to bear in mind that such differentials could be introduced again at some stage in the future.

9.4 Check-list

- Consider whether there might be any obvious restrictions on introducing new activities onto the property, such as through covenants or shared access or services. Check with solicitors too.
- Check arrangements between landlord and tenant, as regards amending the tenancy agreement, granting formal consent, rental and capital arrangements including compensation.
- Take early advice on proposals for option and franchise agreements.
- Take legal advice on creating agreements allowing other parties to occupy part of the property.
- Check what regulations would apply to the new venture.
- Check on tax changes that might arise following the introduction of the new business.

9.4.1 *Sources of information and advice*

- Solicitor
- Accountant
- Local Health and Safety Executive
- Local Trading Standards Office
- Local Environmental Health Division

Chapter Ten

Specifics

10.1 The property

Having assessed the statutory and financial aspects of the proposed new venture, it is as well just to reconsider the basic property features that would be involved in any rebuilding work or change of land use, as alluded to already in section 3.2. The new scheme may have been selected primarily because it appeared to be an attractive business opportunity and without too much regard as to how well the property itself would be suited to it. Conversely, the idea may have arisen because a new use was to be found for a part of the property, such as an old barn or an area of woodland, that was no longer being fully used for farming. In either case, the success of the proposed venture and the feasibility of whether it might be developed in the first place will depend on the way in which the property can be adapted and then the quality of the end product. A farm shop that is visible from the road with easy access and parking and located in an attractive and well lit building will be likely to draw in customers more easily than one that is out of sight at the back of a muddy yard in a dingy shed. The idea of a farm shop may be equally persuasive in both instances and seemingly offer the same commercial potential. The constraints arising from the poorer property would however have to be carefully assessed before going to the more formal stage of drawing up plans and seeking planning consent. On the other hand, finding a building that would seem to have all the features for successful conversion to a farm shop may not in fact be sufficient reason for doing so. This might be if, for example, it were located in a remote rural area with only limited potential for custom or if the owner and his family had little inclination or ability to run such a shop.

These issues may not always be so clear cut. One may look at an old farmyard and envisage that it could be converted to a light industrial use. However, where there had previously been adequate room to manoeuvre tractors and trailers there might not now be sufficient space for turning modern delivery lorries. Also, it may be that some internal walls would have to be removed in order to create adequate working space. If this were then to involve complicated structures with large steel joists, the cost and viability of the whole scheme could come into question. Even if the development were to go ahead, the yard might be situated in such a position that the noise from the converted buildings would affect the enjoyment of the farmhouse. A farmer may be used to carrying out building work and therefore have a notion of the basic costs involved, but premises that are being converted into a non-agricultural purpose may often require a more expensive finish than that which would be acceptable for most farming facilities. It is as well then to check that one is working to an appropriate level of estimated costs rather than be surprised by them at a later stage by which time it may be more difficult to revise or abandon the scheme.

Similar concerns can also apply to an area of bare land being given over to a non-agricultural use. Someone wishing to set up a shooting school may be better advised to do so if there were on the farm an old chalk pit surrounded by scrub or trees than if it were all bare arable land. But if that pit were situated in the middle of fields, the cost and inconvenience of providing access could be prohibitive. Another example would be a farm that is located near to an urban area and might therefore seem to be an appropriate site for a pick-your-own enterprise. However, if it were to be on heavy land that tends to lie wet, it would not only be unsuitable for the kind of crops that are to be grown but would become muddy and unattractive for the visitors.

Essential services may need to be upgraded from those that have been adequate for farm purposes. As farms are generally in open and fairly remote locations, some these services may be costly to provide. Even the track leading to the property can often be many hundreds of metres long and would need to be properly surfaced. Furthermore, 3-phase electricity can be expensive to install if it has to be brought over a long distance. In such situations, domestic drainage has to be by a private system as there is no main drainage in most rural locations. If the number of people on the property were to be increased, larger systems would have to be installed, not only to provide for the greater usage but also to meet the various hygiene regulations. There could be new additional features to budget for too, such as building in ramps for disabled access in order to satisfy those regulations, as well as fire prevention and other measures. Even the telephone line, which is normally taken so much for granted, may need to be upgraded when former farm buildings are being converted into office accommodation, as the existing connection might not be adequate for modern commercial telecommunications.

It is important therefore to identify at an early stage those features on a property that could give rise to additional costs or might even prejudice the viability of the scheme altogether, before then embarking upon more formal assessments or investigations. One should also be ready to look forward beyond the initial stage, even before one may have decided to go ahead! Developments on farms are often done within traditional yards and buildings that were designed for a bygone purpose. As such they have a style and charm that appeal to certain users, but they can also have their limitations particularly as regards future expansion. It is more than likely that a scheme will be initiated on a manageable scale that can be financed and marketed without too much difficulty or risk. Once that has been achieved, it is probable that one will want to build on that success and extend the original facility and thereby also gain a better economy of scale. This could only occur if there were an adjacent site on which the extension could be built and on which one could be sure of gaining planning consent at the time. It would be as well then to check at the outset that there would not be some physical or other constraint against expansion.

10.2 Location

Some of the more immediate issues arising from the particular location of a property have been mentioned in section 3.3.3 and also in chapter 8 on planning regulations. It is of course a fundamental factor in any property matter and there are a number of points that deserve further mention.

10.2.1 Planning

The fact that the planning and highways authorities may be prepared to approve a proposal to convert some part of a farm to another use does not in itself then mean that the property is well located for that purpose. Their approval implies only that the application does not infringe existing policy and is not unsuited to the area around it and does not create unacceptable traffic problems.

It does not normally however give any consideration as to whether the project is best placed to succeed. That will depend on so many other factors, as outlined throughout this book, but including some locational features as mentioned in the sections below.

It may be of course that planning permission would be refused because the property lies in an area where such developments are prohibited. A farm that is situated within, for example, a National Park or Green Belt would be far more restricted in what alternative developments might be carried out there than if it were in a less protected area. To that extent location will be a crucial factor.

Even where there are no such constraints upon the property itself, planning can still have a bearing upon the success of a new venture. If some other development were permitted within the immediate vicinity of the farm it could change the nature of the area. The construction of a major by-pass road could alter the access to a farm or spoil its rural character, so that it would be less suited for other uses that depended upon a setting in the peace and quiet of the country. On the other hand, the expansion of a residential area nearby could increase the potential viability of a commercial enterprise such as a farm shop or pick-your-own operation.

There could also be an overall change in a particular district, if new industries are brought in which attract a larger and more affluent population, bringing new demands on the countryside, whether for pony paddocks or golf courses. A farm located in such an area would therefore find that the developing local economy might create diversification opportunities that would not previously have been viable.

10.2.2 *Catchment area*

Any scheme that depends on visits from members of the public must be in a location that can draw easily upon sufficient numbers of such potential customers. In many cases this will be from within a relatively small local radius. Generally people will be unwilling to travel too far merely to buy something from a farm shop or to have their horse in livery. If the property is remote from the local centres of population, the chances are that the public would anyway be able to find the same facilities on other farms nearer at hand. In other cases, however, the catchment area is differently defined. Holiday accommodation or pony trekking do not have to be near large towns, and indeed it would be counter productive if they were. Instead they need to be located in areas that are popular with and accessible to an appropriate range of visitors. It would be harder to offer farmhouse holidays on the banks of the Mersey than along the River Spey, to use two random examples of locations that are in totally different catchment areas.

A business that does not depend on receiving visitors or commercial tenants, such as a mail order company, is of course more able to be run successfully from a much wider range of locations.

10.2.3 Access

Some reference has already been made to the question of access, particularly in the context of planning in section 8.1.7. Rural properties are by their very nature often approached through minor country lanes and even private tracks. These have changed little over the years even though the volume of local traffic and the size of vehicles have increased so significantly. Where this has involved farm machinery, the increase has so far generally been tolerated. Tractors, delivery lorries and milk tankers have become much larger, and also farm machinery itself is now being driven over larger distances. Farms have expanded in recent times and have often done so by taking on land that may be offlying to the original holding. It is not unusual therefore for tractors and their equipment and even for combine harvesters to be driven for some miles along public roads to reach this additional land. Sometimes this may involve the further inconvenience and disturbance of passing through the centre of villages.

Any proposal for introducing further traffic to and from a farm in connection with a new non-agricultural enterprise could therefore meet with opposition, both from the local community and from the planning and highways authorities. If the public access is deemed to be inadequate, it could lead to a refusal of planning consent or a restriction on the numbers of people using the new facility or the times of day during which it might operate.

Even where there is not likely to be any disturbance of this kind, one needs to make sure that the access is suited to the kind of business that is being established. Visitors may be unwilling to find their way down a series of narrow and probably muddy lanes in order to reach the property. This would be especially true for users of commercial offices, and of industrial units to which delivery vans and lorries would need access. It could also apply to situations where the visitors are ostensibly looking to be in a quiet rural setting, such as for holiday accommodation, but might be put off if they find it is too difficult to reach.

10.3 Management

It became clear in chapter 2 that the most common reasons for diversification tend to arise from either a need to improve income or because the property allows one the opportunity to introduce some new activity. It is less likely for farmers to embark upon a non-agricultural venture because they feel that they have a particular ability or interest in it that they wish to exploit. The future management of the business does therefore often need to be carefully considered.

The principle of diversifying on economic grounds is a perfectly valid one; the big tobacco companies have also, like farmers, faced a steady decline in their core income and therefore diversified into completely new sectors such as insurance. They have been able to do so however with resources that have enabled them to buy in existing operations together with the necessary expertise, which would not normally be the case in farming.

Individually too, farmers are not usually experienced in commercial business management, marketing or even communicating much with the public. All the ingredients for diversification might be in place in terms of the property, the necessary finance, planning consent and a well researched market potential, but it is also necessary to check that the whole project will be well managed. Someone may be a good farmer and furthermore demonstrated great enterprise and imagination in putting together the diversification proposal, but this does not guarantee that he will have the required management skills. These may then need to be acquired, either through training or by bringing in someone who has already worked in that sector. Training may be undertaken either in a business studies environment or through the rurally orientated Lantra National Training Organisation at Stoneleigh, but even this will not ensure that one is well fitted for the new task or indeed that one is going to be able to dedicate the necessary time to it.

Depending on the circumstances and on the scale of the operation, it is likely that some outside help will be needed. For example, the conversion and letting of old barns would be facilitated by using a chartered surveyor to deal with the planning regulations, the building works and the formalities and marketing of the leases. Also when running a farm shop, someone with retail experience would be better able to deal with such tasks as ordering stock, arranging contracts with suppliers, fulfilling all the hygiene regulations and being constantly nice to the public! It has to be recognised too that such help and advice will be most needed when the business is just starting which is just when it may be hardest to make the commitment to fees and wages.

Diversification on a farm will be different to most other businesses in that it can be situated within or close to the home. It may also often involve several members of the family who will therefore need to have the same aptitude and commitment as the farmer himself. The family may be used to living and working together contentedly on a farm but may find it all very different when faced with a constant stream of outside visitors or a yard full of precious ponies.

10.4 Professional advice

There are many aspects of setting up and running a new venture in which one could not expect to be sufficiently competent oneself. Much can be learnt from discussions with other farmers or with the local planning office or trade organisations, but there will come a stage too when it will be sensible to take the appropriate professional advice.

On the financial aspects, the bank will be able to offer some of its considerable experience in such matters. On many other matters a land agent or chartered surveyor can help with preparing outline plans and applying for planning permission, although this can also be done by an architect or planning consultant, depending upon the scale and circumstances of the project. The agent will also be able to point to the tax, insurance and legal issues that are likely to arise although at a certain stage these matters would no doubt be referred to one's accountant and solicitor and the insurance broker. It may be the agent too who will be able to identify specialists who might be required, such as an architect or marketing consultant, and to apply for whatever grants may be available.

The trend towards converting agricultural property to alternative use has been growing steadily, but the market for such premises is inevitably rather fragmented. A national agency has now been set up specifically for such cases and to provide a link between owners and potential occupiers. It is known as The Rural Property Database, details of which are given in the Appendix.

Professional services attract fees and it is an understandable instinct to try to save such expenditure if at all possible! That cost may have to be accepted as part of the investment and indeed when bearing in mind the scale of commitment that is often being made when embarking upon a diversification scheme, it would seem irresponsible not to have had these various important aspects dealt with properly.

It should be remembered that those planning a rural diversification may well be doing so under a particular disadvantage, in that farming is a relatively isolated industry. There may not be someone at hand with whom one could discuss such plans or share useful information and experience. To that extent, involving a professional adviser at an early stage could provide some necessary and informal help in defining the best way forward.

10.5 Security

Farmers and landowners are already well aware of the increasing need to protect goods and property against theft and damage, even in the most idyllic rural area. Gone are the days when the farmhouse door would never be locked and when machinery could be left out in the fields overnight ready for the next day's work. This possible threat of burglary can unfortunately become greater as more people come on to the farm in connection with a new business venture. Not only is it more difficult to control who comes on to the property but the fact that there is another business there may suggest that there will be more items worth stealing, whether office equipment or cash and goods in a shop or warehouse. Not only, as mentioned just previously, will the farmer and his family have had to prepare themselves to welcome strangers on to their property as legitimate visitors, but they will also have to be ready to identify those whose purpose may be unwelcome!

One needs to prepare for this, both as an on-going feature of life on the farm and in terms of installing the appropriate security. This could involve such features as new locks and automatic lights, as advised by the insurers or by the local crime prevention officers, but it may also need a change in some of the existing arrangements.

The dog chained up in the yard has been a familiar sight on so many farms and acts as a good vocal alarm. Visitors, however, who may think of dogs only as pets and even as 'man's best friend', may not be used to the idea of a dog being part of the working environment of a farm and could well object to seeing one chained up and barking at everyone who approaches.

10.6 Check-list

- Look carefully at the physical features of the property and assess the extent of changes that will need to be made when introducing the new venture. Consider also whether there will be sufficient scope for future expansion.
- Check also the implications of possible future changes to the surrounding area and local economy.
- Consider the implications of having the public entering the farm and the need to be able to manage people as well as the business.
- Seek professional advice in matters that are outside one's own experience or expertise.

10.6.1 Sources of advice and information

- Local council
- Land agent
- Solicitor
- Surveyor/architect
- Insurance company/crime prevention officer

Chapter Eleven

Future Trends

Most diversification schemes will have incurred a significant investment in time and effort as well as money. They may also have involved irreversible changes to the structure of the farm. Such commitments can only be justified if it can be reasonably assumed that the new ventures will remain viable for many years. One needs therefore to consider as best one can how things will evolve during that time and how the project would be affected by future changes. This will depend on not only the specific local conditions surrounding the individual property, as considered earlier in chapter 3, but also the overall economic and political trends.

11.1 Agriculture

Diversification implies a switch away from conventional farming. Where this is being done in order to improve on the declining returns from agriculture, as discussed in chapter 2, the further outlook for agriculture will be crucial. After all, one might not be so ready to replace part of the farming business with a new and untried venture if one could reasonably expect that agricultural incomes would be likely to improve again in the foreseeable future. On the other hand, if it were clear that such incomes were going to get even worse over the coming years, one might be more convinced about taking the step of starting up a secondary venture.

Farming in Britain is dominated by the CAP and the World Trade Organisation (WTO). With only few exceptions, most agricultural businesses are dependent on price structures and subsidies that are ultimately controlled by these two institutions. There is at present little reason to expect that this might change. It seems generally accepted that food production in the developed world will continue to be over supplied and that the cost of maintaining subsidised systems as a cushion against low prices will become prohibitive and politically unacceptable. This will become even more crucial as the CAP prepares to face the additional cost of including the former east European states within the membership of the European Union.

Agricultural subsidies and support payments must therefore surely be reduced during the next few years with the result that the industry will be forced to work more towards world market prices and so suffer an overall fall in returns. There may of course be some years when there might be exceptions to this trend, both across the board or for individual sectors, whether due to temporary imbalances arising from poor harvests in major producing areas such as the USA or to changes in consumer demands. In the longer term one may assume that the growth in population and the more even distribution of economic resources especially in the developing world could produce higher prices, but in the meantime one has to accept that basic farm incomes will come under further pressure.

There certainly seems little reason to anticipate any turn of events that might yet reverse this downward trend, other than possibly a major upset in the international currency rates. If agricultural incomes seem unlikely then to improve over the coming years one may feel more readily justified about entering into a scheme that involves replacing part of the farm business with an alternative venture. At some stage no doubt the situation will change and farming may become more profitable again. One ought to consider whether the resources given over to diversification could then be returned to agriculture or whether the process would in effect be irreversible. It is difficult, for example, to envisage circumstances where land that has been converted at great expense into a golf course could be taken back into farming. With some other developments, such as those involving a new use for the farm buildings, the question of reverting to agriculture would be essentially one of financial expediency rather than of physical constraints. However, while it seems clear that farm incomes are likely to continue to decline, more farmers and landowners will look towards diversification. Competition among such schemes will then increase and each developer will need to be satisfied that their own project could be expected to remain viable under that changed scenario. One's assumptions about how agriculture will perform in the longer term could therefore lead to differing conclusions depending on the circumstances. There may be implications also as regards the rural property market and valuations, that are considered in section 11.3 below.

11.2 Rural policy

On the other hand, the fact that the political and economic outlook for farming is so discouraging does not necessarily guarantee that the climate for other rural enterprises will be any better. At present the emphasis does seem to be on encouraging non-agricultural ventures, as indicated in chapter 1, due to changing planning policies, subsidies and social requirements. One has to ask, however, if these factors are likely to continue or whether they might yet be curtailed in some way. It could be, for example, that planning principles will change and that there would be a reaction against commercial developments in the countryside and an insistence instead that farmland be used for more environmental purposes. Latterly indeed the British Government has encouraged the use of so-called brownfield sites for redevelopment in preference to allowing new building on bare land or "greenfield" sites. If such a policy were to be rigorously upheld, it would become more difficult in future to gain permission to set up new schemes in the country and one might therefore be more inclined to proceed now while it seemed still to be feasible to do so. Alternatively, if the general policy were still to encourage other forms of rural development, it could lead to an oversupply and a consequent weakening of the commercial return as other similar schemes are set up in competition in what is generally a rather limited business environment.

It should be noted too that there has over recent years been a marked change in emphasis in planning policy in Britain. Previously, there was a presumption towards protecting agriculture, following a period when food production was an important priority. This was of such significance that it even gave rise to the system of Land Classification, as mentioned in section 8.1.4. More recently, however, planning decisions in rural areas are determined more by the principle of protecting the countryside rather than farming and the constraints on developing good quality land have been modified accordingly.

The full consequence of such changes will depend as much on local circumstances as on the national policy issues, but it will none the less be important to weigh up the overall situation. For example, a planning regime that encouraged the conversion of farm barns might create development opportunities for a wider number of landowners. However unless demand were for some reason to increase accordingly it could result in an overall fall in rents and prices as supply exceeds demand. In specific instances, a venture such as a conversion into a farm shop could be ruined if another were allowed to open in a more attractive, and competitive, position in the locality. There are many trends evolving within the country that could have a direct impact on non-farming schemes that might currently be in preparation. A growing concern for animal welfare could affect the success of introducing an exotic breed to a farm. Similarly, the apparent public reaction against field sports could in time undermine plans to set up a shooting school or to stock a fishing lake. The fact that most rural based enterprises depend upon being accessed by cars makes them vulnerable to transport policies and to the consequences of the failure of such policies. As private motoring becomes increasingly expensive and if public transport were to be improved, it might become more feasible again to commute in to a town centre rather than be expected to drive across country to a workplace in a relatively remote rural setting. While local and current conditions are the most crucial factors to be considered, it will be important to consider the wider outlook too.

Farming in Britain has become accustomed to being dependent, first, on the political balance within Europe and in the rest of the world, and, second, on the vagaries of the climate and on the basic rule of supply and demand. When branching out from agriculture, one may expect to be participating more directly in a world of free commercial enterprise and be less subjected to controls and regulations. There are however instances when such ventures would be directly influenced by changes in Government policy. For some this might be due to a financial dependence in the form of regular grants or subsidies.

The development of wind farms, for example, has been possible only through a commitment by the Government in the Non Fossil Fuel Obligation that enables the power companies to pay a premium price for electricity so produced. This commitment is made for a specific number of years at a time so that the developer of the wind farm can anticipate an adequate return on the initial costs. It would be important however to determine whether at the end of that term the subsidy would be renewed or whether perhaps electricity prices may have risen to the equivalent cost of that generated by wind. If not, one would have to try to structure the venture so that either the investment will have paid for itself by that time or that it will by then at least be able to service itself at the prevailing unsubsidised price.

In most cases, however, Government policy would be more a matter of regulatory control than financial support. These policies could become either more restrictive or more liberal and each would have its consequences. It is possible that the current need to encourage alternatives to farming may in future be countered by tighter restrictions on non-agricultural activities in the countryside, for the sake of conservation. If that were so, those who had been able to carry out some diversified development before the introduction of restrictions would find themselves in a relatively unchallenged position to attract the available demand. If on the other hand, the official response was to give greater encouragement to such activities, then the market could become oversupplied and prices and returns would fall.

It is therefore necessary to look as best one can at how policy is likely to evolve both locally, under the planning authority, and at a national level such as through the proposed rural development measures.

11.3 Market considerations

One needs to consider also how the rural property market is likely to evolve within these various policy frameworks. Diversification is mostly seen as a means of providing an improvement in annual income but it can also be an important step towards preserving or enhancing future capital values. As circumstances change so too does the demand for particular types of property. The impact of falling prices can sometimes be mitigated by spreading overheads across a larger area so that there is an incentive for some farmers to buy in extra land even at a time of recession. The advantage of gaining such economies of scale can mean that these farmers may even be able to pay a premium price for such additional parcels of land. This might be necessary when such land is in limited supply or particularly well located. This same situation is less likely to arise however in areas where the farms are traditionally of a smaller size or on poorer quality land. In other locations, the land market will be supported by a strong demand for properties that have residential or sporting or amenity elements. Within the current outlook then it would seem that, as a general rule, future values will depend upon whether a property has those characteristics that are being sought after.

One cannot change the location of the farm or the quality of land, but it may be that one can increase the level of potential demand for the property by having introduced some form of diversification. For example, many upland farms come within the category of traditional holdings mentioned above. Their agricultural income is very limited and the local land market is similarly restricted. Some of these uplands are however frequented by tourists. It is possible that where a visitor attraction has been introduced it could enable the farm to be sold to a wider potential range of buyers than if it were purely agricultural and that such buyers would have greater resources than the neighbouring farmers. The same could apply in lowland districts too where there might be perhaps medium sized mixed farms on heavy land. The local infrastructure may mean that farmers would be unlikely to have the resources or the opportunity to buy in land for expansion but there could instead be a requirement for non-agricultural uses, whether commercial or industrial. The property on which some of the buildings may already have been converted to such uses could then be expected to attract a greater degree of interest than if it were a just an ordinary farm holding.

11.4 Buildings

Buildings are often the focus of current diversification schemes. Traditional stone barns and former cowsheds have all survived long beyond their intended agricultural use. We are accustomed now to seeing them converted into residential accommodation or stables. There is however a further generation of buildings that are becoming redundant too, as farms are amalgamated and as machinery increases in size. Farms that may previously have had livestock might now be purely arable but the cattle yards have too low a headroom to be used for the storage of either crops or machinery. Grain stores that were designed with separate bins for the different cereal varieties have inadequate handling capacity for modern systems. Most of these buildings are of a portal framed construction and are often situated close to each other in the centre of the farmyard. Many will have been clad in asbestos, which can be expensive to remove. They certainly have little charm compared to the old tithe barn built of slate and stone and it is difficult to see how they could be converted to attractive rural accommodation.

None the less, they do represent a capital resource that it would be better to utilise if possible as they are not going to be making any contribution to either capital or income while they are empty. In some situations, these buildings are already being rebuilt as office accommodation or are being used for incidental storage purposes such as for caravans. It is possible that in future some of these more modern farmyards will be seen as being part of a contemporary countryside that should be preserved. Planning policies may seek to prevent their demolition and to encourage their conversion to other uses even if at a greater cost and with a lesser appeal than with the older barns.

11.5 Woodland

Woods form a significant part of the landscape whether within farms and estates or as commercial forestry plantations. The long term nature of timber production and the restricted returns from it due to competition from imports have meant that the UK industry depends heavily upon Government grant aid. These grants are also used to encourage smaller scale planting for essentially amenity purposes. Previously, tax concessions provided a further incentive towards tree planting, although these were removed when it became clear that the system was being exploited for extensive conifer plantings on unsuitable sites. There is however a continued commitment to offering grants for the establishment of new woods and for the replacement of all trees as they are felled. These grants are currently aimed at meeting part of the costs of establishment and initial management and apply both to commercial plantings and to farm woods. There are also additional grants available for schemes that offer something for the public good. These cover environmental matters in the form of biomass or coppice production and landscaping and amenity issues such as access.

Tree planting can be considered as an alternative use of farmland, particularly on smaller areas of poorer quality land or even on the better arable fields for which a supplementary grant is payable. It is reasonable to expect that such Government aid is likely to continue, if only because without it tree planting would be no longer viable and would therefore cease, or at least be severely reduced. There is furthermore an intention to increase the percentage of land that is forested which is currently still lower in Britain than in many other comparable European countries.

Even with grant aid, tree planting would not be a profitable form of diversification, although it can sometimes be justified on grounds of improving a shoot or creating a more attractive surround to a property, thereby making it more valuable. The recreational use of woods is also unlikely to produce a significant return. The public are not prepared to pay for gaining access to woods other than if it is combined with special facilities such as paint balling or game shooting. Some field sports have recently been the subject of protests and may be prohibited by legislation. Whilst this has not as yet been aimed at game shooting, there is also a move against the private possession of firearms and this could in time impact upon the sport. If that were the case, then tree planting that is undertaken now with a view to improving a pheasant shoot in the future could prove to be rather fruitless.

11.6 Social trends

Many diversification schemes have been initiated to meet the changing needs of society. A greater mobility and an increase in leisure time and in spending power led to the provision of facilities for visitors, whether as holiday makers or for local shoppers or sportsmen. More recently, the improvement in electronic communications and the growing pressures in urban centres has given rise to a demand for offices and other commercial accommodation on farms. These trends are likely to continue, although they will still be very dependent on location. There will always be fewer holiday makers in the fens of Cambridgeshire than on the coast of Cornwall and there will always be greater demand for out of town offices in Surrey than in Sutherland. There are however other social influences that will have an increasing impact on the countryside and on how it is used.

11.6.1 Access

Increased mobility and leisure time has brought with it also a desire for greater access to the countryside. In policy terms this takes a number of forms, some of which offer potential benefits to the farmer and landowner and others seemingly more restrictive. In the former category, grant aid can be secured when providing facilities for walkers and other visitors through, for example, The Countryside Stewardship Scheme or Woodland Grants. In the latter case there is no direct financial advantage, although it could create opportunities for diversification schemes. Footpaths and bridleways cut across private property and are jealously guarded by those who wish to use them as of right, making it difficult even to have them moved to a route that might cause less interference to the farm. Some rights of way are now defined as being open to a wider range of user than walkers and horse riders, allowing access to motorbikes and four wheel drive vehicles. Now too there is to be free access for walkers to areas of open ground such as moor and heath. None of these is likely to bring any financial return to the landowner as most visitors are not prepared to pay for the opportunity to walk through the countryside. There will however be occasions when the fact that people are attracted to a particular locality might improve the opportunities for developing some commercial facility for them, such as farm shops, tea rooms or pony trekking. The strength of feeling among the public and politicians for having access to the countryside suggests that this is a social trend that is likely to be upheld strongly during the foreseeable in future.

11.6.2 *Environmental issues*

There is also a growing awareness and preoccupation with environmental issues, that tend to be seen as giving rise to constraints on commercial farming practice. The restrictions in such areas as Nitrate Vulnerable Zones and Sites of Special Scientific Interest would appear to bear this out, although such policies can also be seen as giving rise to new opportunities for diversification. Organic farming, farm shops and pick-your-own ventures are all in some degree responding to the public's wish to have natural products. This "green" attitude is likely to become more widespread and to bring with it further regulation of agricultural practices ranging from such issues as the preservation of hedgerows to the perceived welfare of farm animals. A few of these regulations may be coupled with grant payments, such as for organic conversion, but in general they will result in a commercial constraint on the normal management of the land and only occasionally give rise to further diversification schemes.

Sustainability is becoming something of a catch phrase, implying that we should currently be managing our environment in such a way as to be able to pass it on to the next generations without any depletion in resources. This has consequences already for commercial agriculture, such as in the use of fertilisers, and for forestry and could also influence policy on diversification if it were determined that farming resources should not be given over heedlessly to other uses.

11.6.3 The country image

Coupled with this is the image that the "country" is a healthy and desirable concept. Many foodstuffs and articles of clothing, for example, are marketed under that style, such as Country Life butter or Country Casuals fashions. Even eggs produced in a battery unit are described on the supermarket packaging as "farm fresh", although the inside of a commercial poultry house would hardly match most people's vision of a farm!

This is a positive feature when compared to the possible alternative of decrying anything rural as being to do with "country bumpkins" and it must inevitably be helpful when developing facilities on a farm or marketing farm products. The popularity of the country image is borne out too by the number of magazines that are published under such titles as *Country Life*, *Country Living* or *Country Illustrated*.

11.6.4 Diet

Changes in the national diet will have an effect on the farming industry and on some countryside features. This covers two distinct categories; that of being health conscious and inclined to following fashions for particular foods such as organic or vegetarian or low fat, and that of having convenience foods. The former may be a minority of the population, but they do have a significant spending power and have therefore made an impact on the industry. This has given rise to many new on-farm opportunities, notably in organic production and for seemingly healthy forms of red meat such as venison, as well as for free range systems that satisfy people's concept of animal welfare. Undertaking organic conversion or establishing a deer farm, for example, both require a relatively long period of development and investment. It is important therefore that the market for that product should still be available by the time that the scheme has been fully established. One is however faced with two particular areas of uncertainty. First, the trend for such foodstuffs may meanwhile not have grown to the extent that was originally expected or may even have failed entirely and, second, that other producers will have come into the market and caused an over supply. Deer farming, as one example, has met with a more limited demand for venison in this country than might have been expected. Fish farming on the other hand has been in danger of being a victim of its own success as production, and imports, have grown to meet an increasing demand for what has become accepted as a low priced commodity.

The debate about the potential demand for organic and free range foods that are produced to specific standards but at a premium price is a complex one and will depend on many interdependent economic and social factors.

The influence on farming of that other market feature of convenience foods may be less direct. There will be less demand for certain traditional cuts of meat, which may affect the viability of some conventional enterprises such as beef or sheep production. A growing trend towards prepared vegetables and ready cooked dishes could result in the market becoming increasingly dependent on and dominated by the major food processing companies.

11.6.4 Politics

Britain is predominantly an urban population and in political terms the number of voters who live and work in the country are only a small minority when compared to those whose livelihood is in or around the towns. Legislation will therefore inevitably favour the interests of that majority so that the workings of the countryside will to some extent be designed to suit the expectations of the urban population. This tends to include provisions for access and welfare and also for conservation since the image of the country is largely a nostalgic one. In the context of commercial farming this can result in a financial cost as efficiencies are lost through such measures as hedgerow conservation, restricted use of chemicals or animal welfare regulations. But somehow the expectations of the urban majority need to be fulfilled and the resource that they represent may as well be harnessed within the less well off rural areas. As a result, there is political encouragement for creating the necessary facilities, whether through national or European grants or in local planning policies. Many of these facilities will be in the form of farm diversification.

Political influences now derive from a number of different levels, each of which may have their own separate agenda. These now incorporate the local councils, the Welsh Assembly, the Scottish Parliament, the national Parliament and of course the European Commission which has a particular power in matters of agriculture. The population in most of the continental countries is more evenly balanced between town and country than in the UK. This has in the past helped to protect the interests of British farmers but there is none the less an ongoing environmental and welfare agenda that will continue to impact upon the workings of the countryside. The popular conception of Europe and of the CAP in particular is that farmers have over the years been featherbedded through subsidies at a disproportionate cost to the public. This has given rise to a feeling that farmers should now be expected in return to offer some facilities to that public. Much of this may be of an ideological nature to do with conservation but it can also lead to commercial opportunities and diversification. In a political context this whole approach is likely to be formalised through the principle of cross compliance whereby present day grants and subsidies would become dependent on certain environmental conditions being fulfilled.

11.7 Personal considerations

Farming and land ownership have a deep sense of tradition. In many cases the present owners and tenants will have taken over the property from their fathers and are intent upon passing it on in due course to their own sons and daughters. There is a feeling of continuity and an instinct too of maintaining things just as they always have been. Change and innovation in the country are more often a matter of regret than of pride; a new farm building is more likely to be seen first as an eyesore rather than as an achievement. The ploughing out of an old pasture or the reseeding of a hillside will also be viewed with the disappointment that something has been lost rather than improved.

The idea therefore of converting part of the farm or estate to some new and unprecedented use may seem like an act of betrayal or even of failure. After all, the previous generations had managed to maintain the land in what would appear to have been its proper agricultural order even when times may have been difficult, so that it might seem wrong now to abandon part of the farm to some alien purpose such as an industrial or business letting or for a recreational pastime such as golf. In all likelihood, however, this may turn out to be the most responsible step to take, as without it the property might no longer remain viable. Similar changes have had to be made before and although they may generally not have involved non-agricultural ventures, they will have had serious consequences at the time.

For example, in the wide open spaces of eastern England that are now given over entirely to arable cultivation, one can still see deserted crew yards which once housed cattle. In those days, the landscape would have included pastures enclosed by hedges and the farms would still have followed a traditional rotation. Fertilizer would be largely in the form of natural manure and, significantly, the business would have provided a livelihood for several families. Since then decisions had to be taken to dispose of the cattle and to make the stockmen redundant. Fields would have been amalgamated and fertilised artificially and new grain stores may have been erected. As the hedges and pastures were ploughed over, the landscape changed and many cherished things were lost, not least perhaps the pheasant and partridge shoot and the hunting grounds. Cottages would be sold and families dispersed and replaced by newcomers and commuters. At the time, the landowners must have regretted such change, but without it the farms would not have survived to the present day. By embracing these changes they were in fact fulfilling their role of custodianship.

In today's context, diversification may provide the same uneasy opportunity for maintaining a farm. Indeed, in those cases where the younger generation is already involved in the family business, it could well be one of them who argues for diversifying because they see it as being the only chance that they might have for keeping the property together in the future. Not only do certain areas of the farm offer scope for producing a new source of capital and income but they would in all likelihood have no further purpose if they were not redeveloped for these purposes. Converting lovely old barns into houses or offices may offend one's traditional view of the country but in the longer term it could be better to have preserved them in this way than to leave them in an used and probably increasingly dilapidated state.

When some of the great estates first developed visitor attractions, like the lions at Longleat or the motor museum at Beaulieu, they were surely criticised for compromising their heritage and for needless profiteering. Yet, without such ventures these properties would not now be so well maintained and, indeed, there are few

estates that do not now in some similar way make good use of the
resources that they can offer the public. Perhaps the same principles
now apply to the family farm as well; in that the current generation
considers it to be their duty to preserve the farm and to provide
continuity for the future even though in many cases this may no
longer be achievable through conventional farming methods. Seen
in that context it would appear almost irresponsible not to resort to
alternative enterprises as a means of countering the decline in
agricultural returns, given of course that there is the necessary
aptitude and opportunity to do so. Recognising the advantages,
and inevitability, of diversification does not obviate the need for
critical analysis as outlined in chapter 3. Indeed, the introduction of
a new business development on to a farm is now more likely to be
seen as a sign of progress and of success, rather than as the
desecration of the good old traditional ways of the countryside.
However this does not then mean that every farmer should feel
bound to undertake such a project. Just because others have done it
will not in itself be justification for anyone to try the same unless
they have the right abilities and circumstances to do so.

The sense of responsibility that landowners have traditionally
had for the countryside around them has been taken over to some
extent by the planning authorities. It is they after all who control
what development and change may take place in the landscape and
they too who are there to interpret the democratic will of the local
population. If some farmland is given over to an unsightly
development it is the planners who will be the target of complaint
and criticism more than the landowner. This rather rigorous
legislative system may make it easier now for landowners to
initiate plans for diversification where they might have felt
previously that they would not want to be seen as being directly
responsible for despoiling the countryside.

11.8 The changing countryside

The assessment about whether to embark upon a new alternative
venture is generally made on an analysis of the individual
circumstances. This focuses on the continued viability of the
existing farm business under prevailing economic circumstances
and on other opportunities that may have been developed in
similar situations elsewhere or which have been identified as
offering new market openings. It is essentially a matter of

recognising recent trends, especially as to how they may affect an individual enterprise, such as whether a beef herd will still profitable, and of identifying other products or services that are already being demanded in rural areas.

The change in some aspects of the countryside has been great, even within the space of just one generation. The impact of tourism, leisure pursuits and of commercial and residential development has been considerable, as has been the introduction of new farm crops. The vivid yellow of oilseed rape was virtually unknown in Britain thirty years ago and the blue of linseed is an even later introduction. Such concepts as "pick- your-own" and "pay as you ride" were also quite unfamiliar and golf was still a rather exclusive pastime. Whereas these innovations are now quite common place in many parts of the country, there are other areas where less change has occurred. This may be due to climatic or locational reasons and also to the attitude of farmers and landowners. Oilseed rape or vines, for example, cannot be grown commercially in northern Scotland. Tourists might find the mining district of, say, South Yorkshire less appealing than perhaps the Moors or Dales a little further north.

These less suitable locations are anyway likely to be the less economic ones. Where there is only limited demand for whatever reason then the price that people will pay will be lower than in the more popular areas, whether as a commercial rent or for bed and breakfast accommodation, for example. The costs of providing the facility, both in its construction and its management, will tend however to be similar in all situations resulting in a lower return for those in the less favoured places. This might be compensated in some degree by the fact that property values would be lower in these latter cases, although that would only be of actual benefit if the new venture involved buying in a parcel of land or building for development purposes.

Some of these circumstances are however changing in themselves. New industries replace the old and bring new development and new populations with new requirements. The coal mining areas in Nottinghamshire and Derbyshire are examples of this, resulting in a visible transformation of the countryside with residential development, pony paddocks, golf courses and other outdoor leisure facilities. How different too are the opportunities now for landowners in north Buckinghamshire compared to about 50 years ago, due to creation of a complete new town at Milton Keynes. Even in the more remote and traditional areas there is change, arising from new attitudes among the younger generation as well as from the increased mobility of the travelling public and a growing desire to "get away from it all".

Where the conditions are such as to encourage viable diversification, one may expect it to become a growing trend. Farmers will be needing the alternative income and the public will have become increasingly accustomed to this sort of change taking place in the rural communities and landscape. The planning authorities too will tend to be supportive although probably still imposing restrictive measures to protect historic buildings or fine landscapes and to limit any unreasonable traffic flow. This may however tend to be concentrated on the better suited locations and so raises questions as to the future of those other areas where such opportunities have been rather restricted. It is often in these more difficult areas that the added income and activity from diversification would be most needed. Many of the poorer farming districts have no alternative but to depend on the very limited incomes produced from hill grazing. The land is too difficult to permit any other form of agriculture and the locations may be too remote or too bleak to attract much demand from tourists or commercial users. It is however in just these sorts of situations that the input from diversification would be so valued. Some change may occur through improved communications and the changing attitudes of both farmers and visitors as mentioned just previously, but there will always be serious limitations too. Those people escaping the more crowded areas will be limited in number, as otherwise their quest would become rather self defeating. The individuals among them will furthermore be more frugal than their counterparts in the more popular places. One can imagine that visitors to the Cumbrain fells spend far less while on holiday than those at the nearby seaside resorts of Blackpool or Morecambe. There can be seasonal disadvantages too. A growing number of tourists may be taking advantage of improved roads and other facilities so as to visit Scotland. But this will be concentrated on the spring and summer and not when it is dark and snowy in the winter. The opportunities for visitor attractions are more limited than in, say, the Home Counties where these businesses may stay open all year, even to the extent of selling Christmas gifts in the farm shop or offering pick your own leeks and brussel sprouts!

The more remote areas can also suffer an element of political ambivalence too. On the one hand there is every intent to support these communities with national and European grant aid that provides both income support and development funding. On the other hand, the landscapes in which they lie are often within special designations such as National Parks or Areas of Outstanding Natural Beauty or SSSIs. These designations lead to restrictions on planning policies resulting in limitations on the new developments. An application to convert an old farm building in a National Park could easily be refused entirely or made subject to a condition that the new work be done in traditional materials. This either denies the farmer the sort of opportunity that would be available to someone in a less precious environment or makes it more expensive through having to build in stone and slate rather than modern steel or concrete. That added costs will not only be harder to fund but will also put an extra burden on a venture that may anyway be attracting relatively limited income due to its location, as mentioned just previously.

There are other situations where diversification will be less frequent and less viable but where it will also be of less consequence to the farming community. It has already been mentioned that the fens of eastern England attract fewer visitors than the coastal hinterlands of the South West. The quality of the land in the east and the scale and potential of the farming that it supports does however mean that there is far less need or occasion to turn to other forms of business. The income from, for example, bed and breakfast accommodation will make less impact upon an intensive Grade 1 arable operation than it would on a mixed farm in mid Wales. This is not only because of the relative scale and profitability of the farms but because there might be less call for such accommodation in the fens than in the more picturesque landscape of Wales.

11.9 Conclusions

The present trends point to an increasing need, and opportunity, for on-farm diversification. For those who have the chance to do so, it would seem unreasonable and even irresponsible not to embark upon some suitable alternative venture. The more crucial question would in fact be what action should be taken by those farmers who do not have this option, due to location or other circumstances as described in chapter 3. Diversification has been in part a response to a new and growing demand for commercial, residential and leisure facilities in the country. It has also of course been a means of countering the continuing decline in farm incomes and of building a broader business base for successive generations. Where this cannot be met by non-agricultural measures, other changes are likely to occur, such as intensification of the farming system or amalgamation with a neighbouring holding. The former can have consequences upon the landscape and upon the workforce and the latter may lead also to redundancies and to houses being sold to non farmers. At worst it could result in farmsteads being abandoned and to certain areas being deserted by the younger generations.

This is not a new scenario but one that is becoming steadily more serious as the agricultural economy deteriorates and as political support weakens. Some farms will become larger and be managed by increasingly commercial methods. Others will become part time holdings where the farmers and their families take on work elsewhere. In the more remote areas where neither of these options are available, survival will be dependent increasingly on grant aid. The trend towards diversification will however become more widespread as more people spread into the countryside and as communications continue to improve. The rural economy will itself become more diverse with farming being just one part of the total infrastructure. It is however the farmers and landowners who hold the basic ingredient from which all this will grow, namely property, and it is they who will therefore have a particular contribution to make to all these new developments.

Bibliography

Haines, Michael. *Marketing for Farm and Rural Enterprises*. Farming Press. 1999.

Nix, John. *Farm Management Pocketbook*. Wye College Press. Annual.

Powell, Elizabeth and Taylor, Derek. *Directory of Rural Organisations*. Farming Press. 1997.

Slee, W. *Alternative Farm Enterprises*. Farming Press. 1987.

Small Food Business Handbook. MAFF Publications.

Thompson, K (ed). *Food and Farming Source Book*. Avebury Publishing. 1995.

Williams, John (ed). *Farm Development Review* Chesterton Publications. Monthly.

Winter, Michael. *Rural Politics. Policies for Agriculture, Forestry and the Environment*. Routledge 1996.

List of Trade Organisations, Government Agencies and other Sources of Information

Alternative Technology Centre
Centre for Alternative Technology, Llwyngwern Quarry, Machynlleth,
Powys SY20 9AZ
01654 702400

British Association of Golf Course Contractors
Angel Court, Dairy Yard, High Street, Market Harborough,
Leicestershire LE16 7NL
01858 464346

British Association for Shooting & Conservation
Marford Mill, Rossett, Wrexham, Flintshire LL12 OHL
01244 570881

British Christmas Tree Association
12 Lauriston Road, London SW19 4TQ
0181 946 2695

British Commercial Rabbit Association
Fairfield House, Sound, Nantwich, Cheshire CW5 8BA
01270 780248

British Deer Farmers Association
Old Stoddah Farm, Penrith, Cumbria CA11 ORY
017684 83810

British Franchise Association
Thames View, Newton Road, Henley-on-Thames,
Oxfordshire RG9 1HG
01491 578049

British Herb Trade Association
164 Shaftesbury Avenue, London WC2H 8HL
020 7331 7281

British Horse Society
British Equestrian Centre, Stoneleigh, Warwickshire CV8 2LR
01203 696697

British Institute of Golf Course Architects
Merrist Wood House, Worplesdon, Guildford, Surrey GU3 3PE
01483 884036

British Organic Farmers and Growers Association
86 Colston Street, Bristol BS1 5BB
0117 929 9666

British Trout Association
8/9 Lambton Place, London W11 2SH
020 7221 6065

British Wild Boar Association
Fen End Cottage, 30 Fen Road, Milton, Cambridgeshire CB4 6AD

British Wind Energy Association
26 Spring Street, London WC2B 6EX
020 7402 7102

Camping & Caravaning Club
Greenfields House, Westwood Way, Coventry, Warwickshire CV4 8JH
01203 694995

Caravan Club
East Grinstead House, East Grinstead, West Sussex RH19 1UA
01342 326944

Clay Pigeon Shooting Association
Earlstrees Court, Earlstrees Road, Corby, Northamptonshire NN17 4AX
01536 443566

Countryside Agency
John Dower House, Crescent Place, Cheltenham, Gloucestershire GL50 3RA
01242 521381

Countryside Council for Wales
Plas Penrhos, Fford Penrhos, Bangor, Gwynedd LL57 2LQ
01248 385500

Department of Agriculture Northern Ireland
Dundonald House, Upper Newtownards Road, Belfast BT4 3SB
01232 520100

Development Board for Rural Wales
Ladywell House, Newtown, Powys SY16 1JB
01686 626965

English Nature
Northminster House, Peterborough, Cambridgeshire PE1 1UA
01733 455000

English Tourist Council
Thames Tower, Blacks Road, London W6 9EL
020 8846 9000

English Vineyards Association
Church Road , Bruisyard, Saxmundham, Suffolk IP17 2EF
01728 638080

European Commission
London Office, 8 Storey's Gate, London SW1P 3AT
020 7973 1992

Farm Shop & Pick Your Own Association
164 Shaftesbury Avenue, London WC2H 8Hl
020 7331 7281

Farm Holiday Bureau
National Agricultural Centre, Stoneleigh Park, Warwickshire CV8 2LZ
01203 696909

Farm Retail Association
164 Shaftesbury Avenue, London WC2H 8HL
020 7331 7281

Farmers' Union of Wales
Lys Amaeth, Queen's Square, Aberystwyth, Ceredigion SY23 2EA
01970 612755

Food From Britain
123 Buckingham Gate. London SW1W 9SA
020 7233 5111

Food Standards Agency
Ergon House, 17 Smith Square, London SW1P 3JR
0171 238 3000

Forestry Authority
231 Corstophine Road, Edinburgh EH12 7AT
0131 314 6156

Game Conservancy Trust
Fordingbridge, Hampshire SP6 1EF
01425 652381

Game Farmers Association
Oddington Lodge, Moreton in Marsh, Gloucestershire GL56 OUR
01451 830655

Health & Safety Executive
Information Centre, Broad Lane, Sheffield S3 7HQ
0541 545500

Lantra National Training Organisation
National Agricultural Centre, Stoneleigh, Warwickshire CV8 2LG
01203 696966

Ministry of Agriculture, Fisheries & Food
3 Whitehall Place, London SW1A 2HH
0645 335577

Mushroom Growers Association
2 St. Paul's Street, Stamford, Lincolnshire PE9 2BE
01780 66888

National Association of Farms for Schools
164 Shaftesbury Lane, London WC2H 8HL
020 7331 7200

National Farmers Union
164 Shaftesbury Lane, London WC2H 8HL
020 7331 7200

National Farmers Union of Scotland
Rural Centre, West Mains, Ingleston, Edinburgh EH28 8LT
0131 472 4000

National Farm Attractions Network UK
National Agricultural Centre, Stoneleigh, Warwickshire CV8 2LG
01203 696969

National Mineral Waters Association
British Soft Drinks Association Ltd, 6 Catherine Street, London WC2B 5UA
020 7836 5559

National Rural Enterprise Centre
National Agricultural Centre, Stoneleigh, Warwickshire CV8 2RR
01203 690691

Royal Institution of Chartered Surveyors
12 Great George Street, London SW1P 3AD
020 7222 7000

Rural Business Network
The Boulevard, Kidlington, Oxfordshire OX5 1NZ
01865 845033

Rural Development Commission
141 Castle Street, Salisbury, Wiltshire SSP1 3TP
01722 336255

Rural Housing Trust
Prince Consort House, 27–29 Albert Embankment, London SE1 7TJ
020 7793 8114

Salmon and Trout Association
Fishmongers'Hall, London Bridge, London EC4R 9EL
020 7283 5838

Scottish Natural Heritage
12 Hope Terrace, Edinburgh EH9 2AS
0131 447 4784

Scottish Office
Agriculture, Environment & Fisheries Dept., Pentland House, 47 Robbs Loan, Edinburgh EH14 1TY
0131 5568400

Soil Association
86–88 Colston Street, Bristol BS1 5BB
0117 929 0661

Telecottage Association
National Agricultural Centre, Stoneleigh, Warwickshire CV8 2RR
0800 616008

Ulster Farmers Union
475 Antrim Road, Belfast BT15 3DA
01232 370222

Welsh Development Agency
Pearl House, Greyfriars Road, Cardiff CF1 3XX
01222 222666

Welsh Office
Agriculture Department, Crown Buildings, Cathays Park, Cardiff
CF1 3NQ
01222 825111

Welsh Tourist Board
Brunel House, 2 Fitzalan Road, Cardiff CF2 1UY
01686 626965

Woodland Trust
Autumn Park, Dysart Road, Grantham, Lincolnshire NG31 6LL
01476 574297

Preparing for Diversification

1. Analyse Business:
   - (a) as currently trading.
   - (b) in foreseeable future,
     allowing for anticipated changes in:

     > prices
     > costs
     > grants and subsidies
     > interest rates
     > regulations
     > family circumstances

     if profitable, do sensitivity analysis and continue annual monitoring;
     if anticipated to become unprofitable, prepare for change;
     if already unprofitable, implement change.

2. Identify Potential for Change:
   - (a) within existing farming system (improving efficiency)
   - (b) through changing the farming system
   - (c) by terminating loss making enterprises
   - (d) by seeking additional sources of income

   Quantify possibility of capital being released through sales of stock etc. and consider reinvestment.

3. Assess Opportunities:
   - (a) using aspects of the property
   - (b) drawing on skills and abilities of oneself and other personnel
   - (c) exploiting locational and marketing features

4. Examine Facilities and Resources
   - (a) available finances
   - (b) physical features (land and buildings)
   - (c) personnel
   - (d) market potential (location, likely demand and competition)

5. Check Essentials:
    (a) property (structural and planning)
    (b) legal (access, leases, covenants, tax, etc.)
    (c) timing
    (d) training
    (e) costs

6. Preliminary Market Research

7. Financial Feasibility

    (a) source and terms of finance
    (b) grants
    (c) budgets

8. Create Business Plan

9. Obtain Planning Consent

10. Arrange Finance

11. Commence Work

The Planning Process

1. Participate in Local Plan Review

2. Check current Local Plan

3. Check whether planning permission required

4. Hold informal discussions with local planning office, highway authority, etc.

5. Assess likelihood of planning permission being granted, in context of:

   Development Plan
   physical circumstances
   suitability of proposal and location
   access
   sensitivity and potential objections

6. Discuss with neighbours, and (if appropriate) with Councillors and pressure groups

7. Draw up plans

8. Submit application

- if consent granted:

     check conditions and time scale
     fulfil Building Regulations and other requirements
     commence work

- if application refused:

     assess grounds for refusal and consider whether possible to resubmit revised application;

     if not:

     discuss with advisers and consider possibility of appeal

Index